HUMPING HEAVY

A Vietnam Memoir

Philip Duncan Hoffmann

Acknowledgement

Over the years I would occasionally lose self-confidence while writing my story, but never the interest in finishing it. If not for the encouragement and valuable input from others, this book may never have come to fruition. My sincere appreciation goes out to:

My infinitely patient wife, Linda
Camilla Greene
Elizabeth Gunn
Gary Thomas
Davy Miller
Ray Gandy
Ron Fakler
Jerry Gebhardt
Ron McDaniel
WJJQ Radio Station
And to all Cav Skytroopers I served with, both living and dead.

Contents

Dedication

Foot soldiers.
Grunts on the ground.
Wars are won by you, lost by politicians.
It is to you, foot soldiers past, who fought with honorable intent.
It is to you, foot soldiers present, who must now bear the weight.
And it is to you, foot soldiers future, who will sadly face the crosshairs
that I humbly dedicate this book.

PDH

Introduction

When I returned from Vietnam, I had trouble talking about my wartime realities without getting uncomfortably nervous. I'm guessing most foot soldiers can relate. Other than my wife, few people ever expressed genuine interest in hearing about the losing side of an unpopular war. And so it was, the most extraordinary chapter in my life seemed destined to be a footnote in the family tree.

Years later, America's interest in Vietnam returned. So did mine. In the fall of 1986, I visited the Vietnam War Memorial. On a rainy night, as I stood alone in front of the Wall pressing my hands up against the wet granite, the war came roaring back to me. Repressed memories flooded into my consciousness.

After that experience, I felt a burning need to tell my story. Still, I could not do so verbally. But I could type. I sat in front of a word processor which I like to compare to a good dog: patient, non-judgmental and willing to listen for as long as I cared to tap out my words. Painting my war on the computer screen was tough, cathartic and fulfilling. It was the longest, hardest venture I ever loved doing.

Within these pages are snapshots, drawn from memory and often told with humor in storybook form. Stringing my snapshots together into an accurate timeline of events, dates and locations was not always possible; however, the story's essence remains unaffected.

In my quest for accuracy, I traveled to the National Archives located in Suitland, Maryland where I referenced battalion operational logs and after action reports. Examples are in this book. I also relied on audio tapes and letters I sent home from Vietnam. But what I found most helpful in constructing the timeline came in two important ways: remembering where I served in country at the time of my mental snapshot (I Corps or III Corps), and who I served under at the time.

The people in this book are real, although I changed many of their names to protect their identities. Other names are simply lost to me. My descriptions come from documentation, recollection, interviews, and yes, a bit of guesswork. Any inaccuracies are unintentional.

Finally, no one should expect page after page of battle action. Those books are already plentiful on bookstore shelves. Even though I served in an infantry battalion, and for a time in a rifle company, the shooting war is not the major story I wanted to tell. My story is chiefly about the emotional and physical challenges I faced in Vietnam dealing with both friend and foe, and how I came through those experiences. The best and worst of man surface during times of extremes. Vietnam exposed both in me. I now expose them to you.

In the end, the units and their soldiers moved on—not all the latter on their feet. In the mud and jungle of Southeast Asia they did their best; they gave it all they had. In so doing, they take their rightful place beside their forebears—honored sons, husbands and fathers.

General John R. Galvin

Vietnam War Memorial

October 1986

This classic Indian summer day in the nation's capital lures appreciative spectators onto the National Mall to bask in their shirtsleeves under a full sun and warm southerly breezes. I join their ranks this midmorning, but not for the weather and certainly not for the gathering crowds mingling in front of the Vietnam War Memorial.

Outside the busy walkway lies a stand of oak and sweet gum well into their fall ritual. The area is free of foot traffic due to signs warning intruders to KEEP OFF THE GRASS. I ignore the signs; they are not meant for me.

I step over a single strand of chain and walk within the restricted grounds until an isolated oak catches my eye. I sit up against it, placing elbows on bended knees and with hands cupped to my face in the manner of blinders on a horse. Through balding branches, sunlight dapples the ground, warming late-planted grass, crimson leaves, acorns, and spiny sweet gum fruit. A light breeze kicks up an earthy, familiar scent.

Obedient sightseers crowd the walkways outside the perimeter chain, leaving me to gaze undisturbed at the black granite panels carved into the not-so-distant hill. As I sit in quiet reflection away from human traffic, I notice in the distance two park rangers cross the chain and slowly approach. They are smartly dressed in their green uniforms and smoky-bear hats. The obvious is about to happen. At best, they will escort me back to the brick walkway. That is, if I am to obey.

But I am not.

Having a healthy respect for law and authority, I am yet determined to hold my ground. If these park rangers knew I traveled hundreds of miles on this pilgrimage to honor my dead comrades-in-arms, would they still confront me? If these two peacetime officers, wearing their neatly pressed uniforms and shiny little badges, knew I paid for this small piece of ground upon which I am sitting—paid for it with pain, blood, fear, tears, stinking damp skin under filthy fatigues, rashes, jungle rot, ringworm, blood-sucking leeches, mental distress, and physical exhaustion—would they still order me away? No, this is *my* memorial and I will not budge until I understand why over 58,000 Americans had to die in that war, and how it was I survived.

The two officers are standing over me now. I look up and our eyes briefly meet before I return my gaze toward the Wall. Without a word, they quietly turn and walk back to the path from where they came.

I don't know why the park rangers didn't perform their duty that day...maybe they saw the tears on my cheeks.

In Country

Inside the dimly lit cabin, a planeload of tired military passengers were trying to catch some sleep when the captain announced over the intercom, "Everyone fasten their seatbelts." It was after midnight and maybe a couple hours from our destination of Bien Hoa, South Vietnam, when the commercial 707 jetliner entered a large storm system the captain said he could not avoid.

The plane heaved and pitched violently in the turbulence. Lightning bolts flashed all about us; thunder shook the fuselage. Men clenched their armrests, releasing them only to grab airsick bags. *What irony*, I thought, as bile rose into my throat, *we're all going to get zapped before we even get to Nam.*

After what seemed an eternity, the clouds spit us out into calmer skies near land. A little later in the flight, the aircraft descended and began circling high above the ground. Lights glittered below, but I saw no airfield. Suddenly, illumination flares burst far below the plane, there to guide us onto the now visible runway.

Without telling us in advance, the captain performed a defensive landing maneuver to reduce low-level exposure to enemy rockets. He descended the plane at a far steeper angle than he would have on a normal landing. The ground was coming up fast, and just when I began to think we were in jeopardy, the plane nosed up before its wheels hit heavily on the edge of the runway.

The jet quickly rolled to the unloading area and stopped where portable steps were waiting. Within seconds, the forward door swung open and a sergeant entered the cabin. Over the still whining engines he yelled, "Welcome to the Republic of Vietnam!"

Welcome my ass.

He instructed us to file from the plane and double time it to a string of nearby buses. Hearing this, a guy behind me said we'd make harder targets to hit. *Harder targets to hit?!* Coming to mind were those old newsreels showing World War II GIs dropping like flies on Normandy beachheads.

We bounded down the steps into an all-enveloping tropical air. Thick humidity, the likes of which I was unaccustomed to in Illinois, captured the smells of jet fuel and diesel exhaust. While ground personnel loaded duffle bags onto trucks, passengers filled the buses bound for the 90th Replacement Center at Long Binh, only a few kilometers away. As the convoy sped single file down a dusty road, someone on our bus asked if the heavy wire mesh covering the windows was there to keep us from escaping. He was kidding, of course. Someone else said the screens were there to deflect enemy hand grenades. He wasn't kidding, and I found myself sinking lower in the seat.

Our ride to Long Binh was uneventful and mercifully short. Once there, everyone crammed into a large tent to await instructions. The side flaps were drawn down trapping light, humidity, and a myriad of bugs that flittered around a few bare light bulbs dangling from wooden cross-braces. Following Army tradition, our hosts made us wait for instruction. Eventually, a sergeant gave a brief but forgettable presentation, ending it with directions to our barracks.

Though dog tired, I tossed in bed on my first night in country. I worried that Army personnel would give no more than a cursory look to my records before cutting orders. They really needed to compare my military occupation specialty (MOS) to my former stateside job to see I belonged at a large, rear-echelon post. My former section chief, a Vietnam veteran, told me to expect that type of high-level assignment.

For the past nine months, I was a classroom instructor at Fort Huachuca, Arizona. I taught radio procedures and Morse code to groups of trainees fresh out of basic training centers from around the country. Graduates of the course became radio telephone/telegraph operators, or RTOs. Aside from my section chief, only four classroom instructors taught radio procedures, including, for a short time, Bobby Murcer, star baseball player for the New York Yankees (Murcer would continue his career with the Yankees after his military service). Each of us taught several classroom hours a day, five days a week, from a list of more than twenty lesson plans.

Never did I expect to land such a great job. When the Army drafted me in June of 1967 to serve a two-year hitch, I fully expected to go infantry and fight in Vietnam. Instead, I'm assigned to the signal corps (communications) teaching classes within the backdrop of the Huachuca Mountains southeast of Tucson. Sweet.

After my initial break-in period at the fort, I was given temporary Sergeant E5 stripes over my official pay-grade rank of Specialist E4. With my added clout, I regularly traveled off base with my buddies on weeknights to the small Mexican border towns of Naco and Agua Prieta for cheap beer and other red-light-district attractions. We'd often return to base near dawn, just in time for me to put on starched fatigues and get to work. On weekends I'd ride my 305cc Honda Scrambler motorcycle up to Tucson and troll the bars along Speedway Boulevard. I played hard, but I also took my job seriously and performed well—well enough to be voted instructor of the year over all other course instructors, both military and civilian, by our graduating classes.

I had hoped to remain stateside throughout my two-year military commitment teaching radio procedure. However, there could be no guarantee with a war in progress, though one could predict. When my time to serve in the Army dropped to eleven months, I could no longer commit to a twelve-month tour of duty in Vietnam, unless I re-upped, and that wasn't about to happen. At that point, odds had turned in my favor. Maybe I had indeed avoided going to war.

But sometimes the odds beat you, as in this case; I still got orders for Nam. While brooding over the details of my next assignment, I came across an unexpected perk. The Army allowed me an additional thirty-day leave prior to reporting to Oakland, California, for processing overseas. That further reduced my tour of duty to ten months. Now while ten months sounded a whole lot better than twelve, to be honest, any length of time was too long for my liking.

The problem was, I no longer felt ready for what lay ahead, physically or mentally. Nine months ago, I was ready. Nine months ago, the Army whipped me into shape and indoctrinated me in most things warlike. Nine months later, I'm out of shape and feel less inclined to kill people. That once gung-ho attitude the Army instilled in me had evaporated long ago.

When my oldest brother, Steve, heard about my orders, he came up with an idea to cut my remaining ten months of service to seven. He had heard about an Army program that gave soldiers who wished to return to college a three-month "early out" release from the military. My initial response was, Hey, let's go for it. But then I remembered my college transcripts. They were wretched.

Before my induction into the military, I had attended Southern Illinois University for more than a year. I started out making good grades, but my self-directed double majors in party animal behavior and art—the art of cutting classes, eventually did me in. Over time, my grades slipped to a point where SIU recommended I waste my energies elsewhere. Steve knew that, so why he thought I could successfully petition out of the military—much less a war zone—three months early to further my dubious college education seemed farfetched. Yet, Steve was less pessimistic. He was currently doing graduate work at SIU and offered to research the idea. So I thought, *why not?* After all, who was I to argue with older, wiser brother?

If you're under the impression that I was ambivalent about fighting a war in Vietnam, then I'm making myself clear enough. However, I was in good company. Many good men felt as I did, and many of those well-intentioned young men sent to fight overseas came home in body bags. And what those patriots got in return for their ultimate sacrifices were families who grieved for them, countrymen who denounced them, politicians who paid lip service to them, and a war that history would prove unworthy of their spilt blood. Additionally, those of us who made it home alive found a government that largely abandoned us. As the conflict dragged on, more Americans at home began blaming the warrior for the war, with the worst among them calling us baby killers.

In spite of any reservations I had over fighting in Vietnam, I was still a proud, and somewhat politically naïve, U.S. citizen. I willingly took up arms because my country called (required, actually), and I felt it my patriotic duty to raise my right hand and give oath. Never did I consider dodging the draft by fleeing to Canada. To do so would have dishonored my family and cast shame on me. My country ostensibly needed my service, and I was, therefore, honor bound.

After my restless first night in Nam, camp personnel at the replacement center kept hundreds of soldiers busy processing in and out of country. My group filled out paperwork, exchanged U.S. dollars for military payment currency (MPC), and received our Southeast Asia Theater clothing issue. Everything was olive drab, including towels, handkerchiefs, V-neck tees, even the boxer shorts.

There was plenty of mindless physical work for the enlisted man, but generally, non-commissioned officers (NCOs) were exempt. That included me, because pinned to the sleeves of my new jungle fatigue shirt were those now unauthorized stateside sergeant stripes. Before leaving for Nam, I was to have sewn on my Specialist E4 patches, but I couldn't bear the thought of demoting myself, at least not at that point. Instead, I had planned to remove the temporary stripes somewhere between Long Binh and my final duty assignment. If outed before then, I brought along my invalid stateside orders authorizing the stripes. I figured those old orders, along with a plea of ignorance, would save me from an Article 15 (reduction in rank and pay, restriction to quarters, and more). A court-martial and possible stint in the Long Binh jail (familiarly known as LBJ, our president's monogram) was even less likely. Obviously, any threat to send me to Vietnam was moot, but I did learn of another penalty, called the shit burn. GIs assigned to that disgusting detail had to pull fifty-five gallon drum halves loaded with human waste out from under raised outhouses, pour diesel fuel onto the contents, and light them. Up from the flaming goo would belch black clouds to foul the air.

Shit burn came to mind during a formation one morning. An officer began calling out names, and when he came to Specialist Hoffmann, Sergeant Hoffmann stepped forward. Now anyone with eyes must have caught the irony, and I suddenly found myself up the Mekong without a paddle. Exposed in front of the entire formation, I begged the officer's pardon and inquired if my temporary sergeant stripes were valid until I reached my final duty assignment.

For a brief moment, the officer looked dumbfounded, as if my words didn't register. Then, with baleful eyes, he approached until he crossed that uncomfortable threshold between two men's faces. I steeled myself for one of those classic Army tongue-lashings—the in-your-face, rip-snorting, ear-shattering, veins-a-popping, spittle-spewing, ass-chewing, basic training drill sergeant kind. But rather than go ballistic on me, the officer showed restraint. He was more officer-esque, and by extension, more menacing. "Are you saying…?" "Do you mean to tell me…?" "You want me to believe…?"

His rhetorical rebuke left no room for defense, so I kept my mouth shut and the expired orders hidden lest I further piss him off. Bottom line, when he finished dressing me down, it ended there without additional penalty. So one could say I got off lucky that day, having only to take his shit—and not burn it.

My new orders had me assigned to the 1st Cavalry Division (Airmobile), an outfit I knew little about. But then it didn't much matter as long as the word *division* was in the title. I envisioned myself sitting behind a big desk in a big air-conditioned office operating a big radio inside a big perimeter protected by big guns. Next stop An Khe, division rear located in II Corps (north-central zone) and home to the Cav's administrative wing.

On my final night in Long Binh, I called home with the assistance of the military affiliate radio system (MARS). MARS enabled soldiers to place overseas calls with the help of U.S. relay stations manned by civilian ham radio enthusiasts, who facilitated the connections. One relay station was located at Camelback Mountain near Phoenix, home to Senator Barry Goldwater. The senator was himself a ham radio buff who let volunteers handle the relays, although he sometimes participated when home from Washington. That happened to be the case on the evening of my call, or so MARS personnel told me. The senator facilitated the call between my parents' home and the MARS station in Long Binh. Part of his function was to push the send key when my parents talked, and release it when I spoke. Mom and Dad had difficulty adjusting to saying "over" after speaking, but we managed. Our conversation was too short, and I will admit to feeling a little homesick when we signed off. The only cost of the call was the long-distance phone charge from the senator's relay station to my parents' home in Illinois. They never got a bill. I heard Senator Goldwater generously picked up the tab for all calls anywhere in the United States.

The following afternoon, those of us flying north took buses back to Bien Hoa and boarded a C-130 transport, a large, noisy, four-prop aircraft. The flight plan included a stop at Tuy Hoa Air Force Base on the South China Sea coastline before continuing to An Khe. Possibly due to our late flight out of Bien Hoa, plans changed and we ended up spending the night at Tuy Hoa. The lot of us, maybe one hundred or more, checked in at headquarters (HQ), where a sergeant led us to the mess hall for evening chow. Along the way, he said that after chow we should seek out empty beds in any of several barracks. Any man who failed to find an open bed was to return to HQ for further instructions.

No one wanted to know what the sergeant meant by "further instructions," so everyone hurriedly ate to be among the first out the door. When the first person at our table picked up his tray to leave, others at the table followed. Once outside, someone in our group suggested we work as a team. The plan was to split up, hit separate barracks, and hold additional beds in case someone struck out. I was fortunate to find a barrack with two open beds and put some of my gear on each. Then I went out to find the others. One guy on our team struck out, so I gave him my spare bed, where he piled his gear. Afterward, we all headed to the enlisted men's club (EM) for a few beers.

It was well after dark by the time we started back to the barracks, but we ended up taking a detour. The sound of surf and the smell of salty air lured us to the South China Sea. The beach was grand. We took off our boots and socks and dug our toes into the still-warm sand. Rolling waves and refreshing breezes further intoxicated our dulled minds. Soon we were lying on our backs looking up at the stars, quietly talking about home and drifting toward un-consciousness. The war seemed continents away.

We might have lain there all night had it not been for a secu-rity patrol scouting the beach. They spotted us with their flash-lights. "Who goes there?" one of two security guards shouted. "We're GIs, the good guys," we shouted back. The soldiers cautiously approached. One pointed his rifle in our direction. The other held back an alert German shepherd that was straining at its leash.

The beach was off limits at night, as all those signs we ignored made clear. During the day, the area was open to military person-nel. But after dark, security patrolled the coastline against enemy landings. The guards gave us no time to put on our socks and boots before ordering us away.

Back at our barrack, my roommate and I were in for another sur-prise. Piled outside the front door was all our gear. Inside, a couple of squatters were asleep on our beds. We shook the claim jumpers awake and that led to a shouting match. All the commotion woke up the flyboys and they turned into a pack of growling junkyard dogs.

"These bastards took our beds," I appealed, as if our peers would hold court. Possession being nine-tenths of the law, we lost on ap-peal and came close to losing more than that. The dog pack looked at us like we were scraps of meat. Swallowing our pride, we judi-ciously backpedaled out the door and returned to HQ to seek advice on where to bunk. There on the ground lay the answer: sleeping bod-ies littered the area. I grudgingly carved out a small piece of terra firma, spread out my poncho, and called it a night.

Next morning I woke up stiff and sore from the terra being *too* firma. After re-packing my dew-covered gear, I shuffled off to the chow line and later toured the base before flying to An Khe. Man, those flyboys had it going for them with all that sand and surf to play in. They even had a freshwater swimming pool, volleyball nets, and tennis courts. What's more, Vietnamese hooch girls did their laundry, cleaned their barracks, and scrubbed their real flush toi-lets. It was almost enough to make this Army boy defect to the other side...the U.S. Air Force.

At An Khe we completed our gear issue, which included M-16 assault rifles and rucksack backpacks, or rucks. We also received plastic wallets sporting Cav logos. They had zip lock "waterproof" compartments that held stuff you didn't mind getting wet. All stateside duffle bags were stored in footlockers inside a large warehouse. Hundreds of them were stacked from floor to ceiling along rows of shelving. In a macabre sort of way, they looked like hundreds of small coffins.

Back at the barrack, I donned all my gear and checked myself out. The new jungle fatigues were functional but lacked any fashion sense. They were baggy and sported large pockets. The best of the lot were my new jungle boots. They were sharp looking and lighter than the black stateside issue. The uppers included patches of green nylon that helped the boots "breathe." Feeling all smug in my full military regalia, I assumed a fighting position holding my M-16 assault rifle.

Don't mess with me, 'cause I'm a bad som' bitch.

During all my posturing, I almost forgot that I might actually have to put this fighting gear to use. That sphincter-puckering possibility would remain unknown until after division orientation, or "charm school."

Those of us new to the 1st Cav were ushered onto bleachers adjacent to a large, open field to watch a staggering display of the world's most sophisticated weaponry. Tanks rolled onto the field firing their cannons; armored personnel carriers (APC) fired their .50 caliber machine guns; howitzers showed off their assorted cannon rounds; and helicopters demonstrated their multiple uses, from carrying equipment and personnel to providing potent offensive firepower. I was most impressed with the sleek Cobra attack helicopter. When heavily fortified, it carried enough rockets and mini-guns to turn a small piece of real estate into dust. The combined display was awesome to see, and so I came away with a vast appreciation of the new mechanized cavalry.

Used to be, the word cavalry brought to mind horse-mounted soldiers who used speed and the element of surprise to gain advantage over their enemy. But in more modern times, after the military adopted faster, motorized vehicles, horses went to pasture and the cavalry had to share its reputation with other fighting divisions.

Enter the helicopter with military applications. In 1965, the Air Force and Army reached an agreement in which responsibility for helicopter operations went to the Army. By the time Cav division deployed to South Vietnam in September 1965, it had reestablished its reputation for speed and surprise using helicopters. The Cav had an impressive array, well suited for operating in Southeast Asia, earning the division the monikers First Team and Airmobile.

Before the 1st Cavalry Division (Airmobile) arrived in Vietnam, communist North Vietnamese regulars (NVA) and guerilla Viet Cong (VC, Victor Charles) had been accustomed to moving with relative impunity within jungle strongholds in the south. Shrouded by dense, sometimes triple-canopy jungle, the enemy was hard to spot from the air and equally hard to get at by ground, at least in conventional ways. Running motorized vehicles along scant roads into those areas was difficult and slow, and fixed-wing aircraft needed long runways to land men and materiel. Helicopters, however, required only small clearings to land, and that gave the Cav remarkable flexibility to quickly deploy military assets anywhere the enemy congregated—a trademark of the old cavalry horse soldiers. The Cav soon proved itself worthy, becoming by war's end the most decorated American combat division in Vietnam. It had won decisive victories in some of the war's most intensive battles and campaigns—Ia Drang Valley, Hue, and A Shau Valley, to name a few. I quickly decided this outfit was too gung ho for my liking. Hell, a guy could get killed.

An Khe was not without its creature comforts. It had, among other things, a post exchange (PX) and an EM club. One night I went to the club with a bunch of soldiers for a couple of beers—or was it a bunch of beers with a couple of soldiers? Either way, to my surprise the club had live entertainment. On stage was a South Vietnamese rock group, consisting of three young men and a woman, playing American and British rock 'n' roll. Their heavy accents detracted from their surprisingly fair instrumentals, but as the evening progressed, their vocals sounded better with each beer (I must have had a bunch of beers with a couple of soldiers). Toward the end of night, I reached that height of inebriation when a grown man is likely to put his friend in a headlock, rub knuckles in his scalp, and proclaim with teary eyes, "I love ya, little fucker." Fortunately, none of my stateside friends was in attendance. However, that didn't prevent me from finding another way to embarrass myself. Toward the end of the night, I came up with this brilliant idea (sober translation: harebrained) of offering the Vietnamese band a business deal.

Back in Carbondale, Illinois, my two brothers were in the planning stages of opening a liquor store and a college nightclub. They intended to book live bands, and I thought this quasi-rock group should play at their future club. Never mind the obvious barriers against the idea, such as why my brothers would even give a shit, or how I'd get the group out of Vietnam, or pay their way to the United States. My resolve was unshakable, because, as with all great thinkers under the influence, these were mere speed bumps on the highway of roadblocks.

After the band's last set, I seized my opportunity and knocked on their changing-room door. The door opened only a crack, enough to display one squinty eye. The wary band member used it to glance at me before saying the bathroom was down the hall. I ignored the snub and announced that I had a unique business opportunity to present to the group. The door remained slightly ajar. I went on to say that, present employment circumstances notwithstanding, I was a talent agent for a company in the United States and would the band be interested in playing there? The squinty eye popped open, a clear indication that I now had him by the nuts. He turned to his fellow band members who began chattering in Vietnamese. When he turned back, the door swung wide. Inside, everyone was smiling at me as if rich Uncle Nguyen had come to pay them a visit.

They invited me in and I immediately fished from my Cav wallet the one wrinkled business card my brothers had given me. I must say they looked impressed by it, even though the card read S-T

Hoffmann Enterprises, Inc. and had no reference to a talent agency or me. The omissions were apparently of no importance, for by this point I had them hanging onto my every mumbled word. Minutes later, we struck a deal. Well, almost. There were still those nagging travel and money issues to overcome. I told them not to worry, that upon my return home I would see to them myself.

Business now concluded, I accepted a free drink.

The next morning, my throbbing brain tried to sort out what had happened the night before. I cringed at the thought of having duped the band into thinking they were going to play in America, although at the time it did seem like a good idea. And it was in one respect: I got a free drink out of it. Still, it was a lousy thing to do, but not necessarily shameful.

I mean, so what if these Vietnamese kids received false hope; wasn't false hope better than no hope? With little doubt, they would wake up excited at the prospect of visiting the land of opportunity, to experience real peace, probably for the first time in their young lives. What could be wrong with that? It's good to have dreams, right? Just as it was *my* dream to return home alive with all my fingers and toes. In my mind, we made a fair trade. I gave them hope for a better life, and because they needed me to survive my tour, maybe they would include me in their Catholic or Buddhist prayers.

Regrettably, An Khe was not my final duty station. Division rear cut orders to Phu Bai and the 596 Signal Company. Located in I Corps, Phu Bai was in the northernmost region of South Vietnam, just south of the ancient capitol of Hue. Both were near the demilitarized zone (DMZ), a no-fire strip of land separating the north from the south along the 17th parallel.

Things were getting more interesting.

I Corps

When our C-130 aircraft arrived at Phu Bai, I immediately reported to HQ and watched the desk types glance over my papers. Leaving nothing to chance, I made sure they understood I wanted to operate a bank of radios on base. They made sure I understood that wasn't going to happen.

"Can't use you here, specialist. Jump on the next chopper for Camp Evans and 5th Battalion."

"Fifth Battalion...that's *signal*, right?"

"No, infantry."

Infantry? Holy shit!

No amount of cajoling could change their minds, and thus my circumstances took a sharp turn for the worse. The word *infantry* had a discomforting ring to it. Still, a radio slot at battalion might be okay, as long as it didn't lead to the next level down. That was company level, where the chance of humping the boonies was far greater.

A helicopter loosely resembling the Oscar Meyer Wiener Mobile stood ready to ferry others and me to Camp Evans. The camp was located inside South Vietnam's northernmost province of Quang Tri and closer yet to the DMZ. This being my first helicopter ride in a Chinook, or shithook, I felt a bit uneasy when the twin overhead rotors revved up, making the bird shudder at liftoff.

Camp Evans was a sprawling base camp built on an open plain. It was also close enough to heavily forested mountains to make it vulnerable to enemy rocket fire. The camp had been home to a regiment of Marines until the 1st Cav replaced them during Operation Jeb Stuart that began on 15 January 1968. Military Assistance

Command, Vietnam (MACV) had deemed it important to increase troop strength inside I Corps in response to enemy insurgents coming across the DMZ. Command put the 1st Cav's airmobile, quick-response capabilities to task when it ordered the division to move north from the Central Highlands.

Cav Division was still marshalling its resources within I Corps when the small Marine outpost at Khe Sanh, also located in I Corps, came under siege on 21 January. Ten days later, the countrywide Tet offensive of 1968 began. In I Corps, the 812th NVA Regiment and two VC battalions tried to overtake Quang Tri City. Cav Skytroopers and attack helicopters stopped enemy designs on the provincial capital. Around that same time, the ancient imperial capital of Hue did fall to the enemy. The ensuing fight to retake the citadel went on for weeks. Marines from the 1st and 5th regiments, soldiers from ARVN's 1st Division, and Skytroopers from the 7th and 12th Cavalry Regiments eventually broke into the city where fighting continued door to door. On 24 February, the communist North Vietnamese flag was lowered for good.

Still under siege were the brave Marines at Khe Sanh who were vastly outnumbered and surrounded by the enemy. Cav Skytroopers eventually air-assaulted into the area to help break contact on 8 April.

The countrywide Tet offensive ultimately ended as a strategic defeat for the communists in that they kept no ground. Yet they found unexpected success in another way, and it came in the form of public opinion. Stunning though our victories were, civilians at home were blindsided by the events of Tet. Before the offensive, our government and military officials had led us to believe communist insurgents were losing their ability to wage war. Troop levels were soon to drop, they said. That being the case, Americans wanted to know how it was possible communist insurgents could mount such well-coordinated attacks throughout the south and kill so many of our soldiers. Tet caused more Americans to distrust their government, and so the anti-war drumbeat grew ever louder, even within conservative ranks. Winning battles and killing vast numbers of communists would no longer mollify the masses back home. The

American people expected a quick victory and a return of their soldiers.

Also affecting public opinion were news broadcasts of the war. Shown daily on TV sets across America, the reports were unprecedented in that they arrived only a day or two after the events occurred, and in blood red at the dinner hour. "Pass the mustard, please. I've lost my taste for ketchup." Families at home were having their sensibilities assaulted on a daily basis by the graphic sights and sounds of our young men fighting and dying in a faraway foreign country. And unlike those old Hollywood movie productions depicting the glory of battle, these news broadcasts were gritty reality, not glory filled but gory filled. None ended in final victory for the allies. Instead, they went on and on, like those old weekend serials shown at local movie theaters, each ending with the same tagline, "To be continued."

After the '68 Tet Offensive, the 1st Cav aggressively pursued enemy insurgents. Skytroopers effectively rooted out their strongholds, including the bloody A Shau Valley campaign, coded Operation Delaware, which ended 17 May 1968. By the time I arrived toward the latter part of August, the Cav was generally involved with mopping-up operations.

Up to this point I'd spent most of my time with fellow "cherry" soldiers new to Vietnam, and REMFs (rear echelon motherfuckers). But at Camp Evans, I came in contact with more seasoned infantry foot soldiers, known as grunts. They were usually easy to spot. Not the most social lot to anyone outside their exclusive club, grunts seemed to prefer their own company and were generally independent, irreverent, odorous, and unkempt. Considering the conditions they lived under, how could they be otherwise? Grunts spent most of their days living in the bush humping the boonies as they sought to initiate enemy contact. They faced the constant threat of combat in the field as well as booby traps, menacing critters, and other risks and hardships. Much of the time, they ate out of cans. The commode was wherever they squatted. Usually exhausted by the end of a long day's hump, they slept on the ground in their sweat-stained or rain-soaked fatigues. Perimeter watch always interrupted their sleep, so important to a grunt. And under the veil of darkness, only a tripwire or a keen eye separated him from a slit throat. Knowing all that, I couldn't help but admire the grunts. I also knew I didn't want to be one; the war was already too close for my liking.

My gypsy travels had yet to end. Fifth Battalion HQ decided to pass me to its forward operating base (FOB) a few kilometers (klicks) away. Known as landing zone (LZ) Jack, the small fire support base was located closer still to the mountains. But before moving on, I would have to participate in another orientation. Until then, I walked on base for a couple of days, scuffing up my new jungle boots to make my new-guy status less obvious. Noisy helicopters flew low overhead constantly, and booming howitzers routinely fired harassment and interdiction (H & I) volleys. All suggested a war was going on around me—a war I had yet to experience.

When not walking around camp aimlessly, I pretty much stayed in my two-man canvas tent writing letters home, reading, napping, and avoiding bullshit area detail. Boredom was inescapable, and it didn't help that the GI next to me avoided conversation. Evenings were even less exciting. I once tried taking in a movie shown under a large tent packed with soldiers. After the projectionist threaded a reel onto a 16mm movie projector and pointed the lens toward a makeshift viewing stand, the tent flaps came down, trapping heat and humidity, body odors, and cigarette smoke. The unbearable combination drove me away.

Orientation of all FNGs (fucking new guys) included a day's march and overnight stay outside the camp's perimeter. We'd be humping heavy, carrying supplies sufficient for several days out. This would be my first time on foot beyond a base perimeter carrying a ruck, a loaded M-16, several cans of C-rations, bayonet/knife, flak jacket, utility belt, ammo belt, steel pot over a plastic helmet liner, two canteens of water, mess kit, poncho, poncho liner, extra socks, entrenching tool, water purification tablets, insect repellent, malaria pills, personal hygiene supplies, and more. The weight of the ruck pulled hard against my shoulders, and the steel pot helmet felt awkward on my head. I couldn't imagine adding a radio to the mix. Where was there room on the ruck, anyway?

The night before we were to leave the wire, inclement weather pushed in and postponed our plans. On 4 September, battalion's G-3 operations officer made the following written record in his daily operations report. Numbers ending with H indicate military time based on a twenty-four hour clock. For example, 1515H is 3:15 PM. LP stands for listening post—likely squad or team size—positioned outside the perimeter at night to monitor enemy movement.

> 4 Sep 68:
> 1855H
> weather warning. 5-6" rain. winds up to 40 knots.
>
> 5 Sep 68:
> 0110H
> check all bunkers to withstand coming weather.
> no aircraft available until afternoon.
> 1025H
> keep all LP's out during severe weather period.
> favors enemy ground attack.
>
> 6 Sep 68:
> 1110H
> check all bunkers and report ones damaged, falling or having water in them more than one foot. all aircraft grounded.
>
> 1515H
> be alert for enemy seeking higher ground.

Two days later, the weather cleared sufficiently for us to saddle up. Over one hundred cherries and our veteran cadre marched outside the wire, past Camp Evans's multi-layered perimeter fortifications, all meant to impede enemy ground assaults and night probes. Coils of stretched concertina wire encircled the camp. They looked like giant slinkys covered in razor blades. Tripwires and illumination flares guarded against night probes. And deadly claymore antipersonnel mines, propped off the ground on short metal legs, dotted the wire. Larger than two clenched fists, each device contained 700 steel balls embedded inside a layer of composition C-4 plastic explosive. Soldiers detonated them remotely with the use of a clicker device. Large perimeter defenses also employed 55-gallon drums filled with jellied gasoline, called Phugas. When detonated remotely, flaming jelly made for a hot time outside the old camp tonight.

With the relative safety of Evans falling farther behind us, our group marched single file for maybe a couple klicks from camp. Eying the men around me, I guessed the vast majority had come directly to Vietnam after two months basic training and two months advanced training. They looked fit from their recent months of physical activity, whereas my PT over the past nine months mainly consisted of curling twelve-ounce beers.

As the march wore on under a relentless Southeast Asia sun, sweat poured off me, and my back arched forward from the weight of the ruck. I took some solace in that a few soldiers looked as tired as I felt. When our trek finally ended on a barren hill, we all dropped our gear and looked forward to standing down. But rest was not yet on the agenda. The cadre barked orders for us to form a perimeter and set up camp.

I couldn't participate in setting out trip flares and claymores because my training in radio operations didn't cover those areas. I was, however, eminently qualified to dig foxholes. After expending a considerable amount of energy digging my foxhole with a small entrenching tool, one of my chaperones was nice enough to let me dig his. Later, when everyone had finished digging their holes, the cadre made their inspections and, naturally, gave orders to dig deeper.

Toward sunset, we received final approval on our security measures and foxhole depths and could thus begin serving ourselves dinner. In my C-ration box, I found a small P-38 can opener, or John Wayne, as it was called, and attached it to my dog tags. Trying to open a can with it for the first time was a joke. I thought I'd starve before the lid finally popped off. Also in the box were plastic utensils. I used the spoon to scoop out a bite of whatever. After only a couple chews, I could barely wash down the contents with warm canteen water. So much for that can of mean cuisine, and I reached for a different entrée.

In all fairness, not every C-ration tasted like Kennel Ration. I rather enjoyed the peanut butter, jelly, and crackers when I could get them, and the peaches and pound cake were yummy. The problem was, just about every other soldier liked them, too. We'd sometimes trade parts of meals in the field. Still, it was that rare individual who didn't mind eating the beefsteak *(gag)*, or ham and eggs *(puke)*.

My gut was already hurting without insulting them more with C-rats. The sad fact was I hadn't taken a dump for a few days, and I had always been regular, except for my initial days of basic training at Fort Leonard Wood, Missouri. There, the barracks latrines had rows of toilets closely lined up on two facing walls with no partitions between the crappers. Every morning, I would try in vain to pinch off a loaf while facing men to my front and practically touching knees with men next to me. Now if that wasn't enough to impact one's colon, a drill instructor occasionally stood at the latrine door screaming at us to get a move on (pun intended). Well, not surprisingly, my anal sphincter shut tighter than a duck's ass, then as it had now, and it would stay shut until mind ruled over matter, the matter of similar size to one of those mini Nerf footballs.

The whole business of marching outside camp to spend the night in the open seemed like a ridiculous waste of time. So what if some cherries were a little rusty at setting out trip flares? One night in the bush would surely square them away. And the cadre's harassment was equally unnecessary. This wasn't basic training, for Christ's sake. Their constant reminders that we were in Indian country, visible and vulnerable, began to seem like a silly scare tactic. I'd been in Nam for about three weeks now and neither seen nor heard from Victor Charles. That, however, was about to change, and very soon.

Sunset signaled an end to the workday, and a sense of calm settled over the perimeter. Our final orders were to stay quiet by our foxholes. My foxhole was on the side of the hill not visible to Camp Evans but in clear view of the mountains.

Peaceful thoughts of home and better days drifted over me when a noise sounding like a muffled *pop* came from the direction of a nearby mountain. Seconds later, I heard a distant explosion from the opposite side of our hill in the direction of Camp Evans.

"INCOMING!" shouted the cadre, who were standing on top of the hill.

I jerked my head around in time to see our chaperones scramble to their foxholes. I threw on my steel pot, locked and loaded my sixteen, and rolled into my hole, thankful now for their order to dig it deeper. My initial reaction wasn't so much fear as it was confusion. The explosion wasn't close to our position, which made me think we were part of some kind of training exercise designed to check our responses.

Another *pop* from the mountainside before another distant explosion. From the top of our hill, someone yelled that Camp Evans was under rocket attack. It was then the group of us realized we were not in immediate danger, and like a family of curious prairie dogs, heads began poking out of foxholes.

Another *pop*. And another explosion. The rocket attack wasn't killing me but my curiosity was. I just had to see the effects on camp. So while events distracted the cadre, I, along with a few other soldiers, crawled up the hill to watch the attack unfold.

Looking out at Camp Evans, I could see clouds of dust kick up where rockets exploded. Someone behind me yelled that he could see wisps of smoke coming from the mountains. Apparently, so could the heavy gun batteries on camp, for before long they were returning fire.

The cadre noticed us out of our foxholes and ordered us back. Reluctantly, I returned to my hole. From there I watched our cannons draw a bead on those enemy rocket launchers, pounding them into submission. Soon the rocket launchers fell silent. Then our cannons ceased fire. The shooting had ended, and once again the countryside turned tranquil.

Sleep didn't come easily after I witnessed war for the first time, distant though it was. With little doubt, men on both sides of this ideological divide died over the exchange, and I had to ask myself, to what purpose? Would lobbing a few rounds back and forth bring either side closer to ending the war? The episode reminded me of adults playing the children's game of tag; the mentality was the same, if not the deadly results.

My mind drifted back to my carefree youth and those dog days of summer playing cowboys and Indians with boyhood friends Bill

Roesner and Mike McCarthy. With cap pistols strapped to our legs, we'd shoot each other several times over on any given afternoon. Killing was fun then, and so much safer.

As often happened, though, we'd eventually argue the finer points of the game. "I killed you!" "Nuh-uh, *I* killed *you!*" And so in those circumstances, when negotiations deadlocked because no one could be coaxed into dying, I would simply jump on my phantom horse and ride home to the refrigerator for a glass of ice-cold Kool-Aid.

During those trigger-happy afternoons, I had a measure of control over my life (unless Mom yelled from the window for me to come home) that I didn't have as an adult sitting in this foxhole. Here I was a stationary target, vulnerable to a possible long-range rocket attack. And here, my M-16 would have been as effective as those cap pistols.

Our cadre warned us the attack could be a prelude to one on *our* position, and not for a moment did I consider that a silly scare tactic. However, the night remained uneventful, and the next morning we set about the business of packing our gear and filling in foxholes.

When we returned to camp, I was relieved to see my tent was still intact. In fact, all nearby structures were unaffected by rocket fire. Most of the damage had taken place at and around the ground-based aircraft. Sandbag revetments helped protect helicopters, but some birds still incurred damage. Shrapnel had also ripped through several surrounding tents, but not before most occupants fled safely to underground bunkers. Most, that is, but not all. Five Americans died in the attack. Eight more were injured.

It was business as usual in camp after the rocket attack, in spite of the recent death and destruction. Helicopters were repaired, tents were replaced, the wounded were patched, and body bags were filled. Veteran soldiers seemed inured to the constant dangers, which made me wonder, would I someday be numb to it?

On or about 10 September, I went to see 5th Battalion's adjutant personnel officer to protest my latest duty orders.

"I'm being sent to Alpha *Company*, sir? Not battalion?"

"Affirmative."

"Alpha *rifle* Company?"

"That's affirmative," he said with emphasis.

The reality of my serving in a rifle company was harder to swallow than a C-ration. "So battalion doesn't need an RTO but Alpha Company does, sir?" I pressed him.

"I don't know if Alpha needs an RTO, specialist, but that's where you're going."

He doesn't know if Alpha needs an RTO! What exactly does that mean?

"Sir, what exactly does that mean?"

"It means the company commander will decide your duties and those duties may or may not involve carrying a radio," he said matter-of-factly.

This was well beyond anything I had anticipated. Exceeding proper decorum, I said, "Sir, I'm an O5B2H radio *instructor*."

"Congratulations. Tell me, did you qualify with your M-16?" he asked sarcastically.

Expert, I wanted to brag, but immediately thought better of it.

My voice now rising, I told him I qualified over a year ago and probably wouldn't remember how to field strip the damn thing. I reminded him again that I was an instructor in radio communications and was thus overqualified to be a grunt radio operator and....

"Don't push it, specialist!" the officer warned.

I properly shut up and waited to be dismissed—or slapped with an Article 15.

Possibly because I backed off, the officer dangled a carrot in front of my dazed expression. He said when a battalion job slot opened at LZ Jack—maybe in a couple of months—my company commander might recommend my advancement to a position there. That managed to mollify me somewhat since I was confident in my abilities. I didn't worry about a good recommendation, only that my unconditioned body and bulging waistline (thanks to Mr. Malted Barley and Miss Fragrant Hops) might soon be humping a radio in the bush where the communist bad guys lay in waiting.

So it had come down to this. After three weeks of roaming the country, I finally had a place to hang my steel pot: Alpha Company, 5th Battalion, 3rd Brigade, 7th Cavalry Regiment of the 1st Cavalry

Division (Airmobile). The last great unknown was my exact assignment within the company.

The night before departure to LZ Jack, I wrote a letter on construction paper to Linda Wright, the woman who would one day take my hand in marriage.

10 Sept. 68

Dear Linda,

Here I am on vacation in this glorious land. I can't even make this place sound good. This is my third week here and I still haven't reached my final unit. My travels started in the southern part of Vietnam and have worked up to 15 mi. from the DMZ. The main headquarters for me is at Camp Evans near Hue. From here I'll be going to LZ Jack (LZ means landing zone). This place is out near the jungle. I'm not going to lie to you so I'll tell you like it is. I'm in the 1st Air Cavalry, which is a gung ho infantry unit. My first 2 months I'll be in the field with a radio on my back. Good experience I guess. If things go well in the field my next job here will be at a command post [battalion].

Only one time did I see a sign of war. One night at Evans a company of us slept on a hill outside the camp for training. At dusk the camp was hit with rockets from the Viet Cong. When it was over 5 were killed and 8 were wounded. Needless to say I was scared shitless. I suppose I'd better get used to it, the way things are going for me. I have many things to tell you, some on the lighter side, but I don't have time to urinate around here. When there's a chance I'll write a much longer one. Excuse the stationary, but a person has to make [do] with what he can get a hold of here. I hope you write. I can think of no other person I would rather hear from most.

Always thinking of you –

Phil

The next morning, I packed my ruck and climbed aboard a Huey "slick", the Cav's gold-standard troop transport for moving rifle companies in the field. A slick had the capacity to carry seven or more soldiers, plus the pilot, co-pilot, and two door gunners. Each gunner manned an M-60 machine gun on either side of the helicopter. On this morning, I was the crew's lone passenger. As I sat unrestrained on a canvas bench seat between two large open doors, the crew chief (also a door gunner) reminded me to turn the muzzle of my M-16 rifle down. That way I couldn't accidentally shoot a round up into the motor housing during flight and thereby accomplish the enemy's objective. En route, the gunners constantly scanned the terrain below watching for enemy tracer rounds.

LZ Jack, or Hill 50, was approximately 10 kilometers southwest of Camp Evans and in close proximity to the mountains. From the air, the LZ reminded me of some remote tribal habitat pictured on the pages of *National Geographic*. Bulldozers had cut embankments and pushed dirt on and around the hill's perimeter—dirt that would turn to mud with the slightest amount of rain. Earthen bunkers, covered by corrugated metal and sandbags, dotted the perimeter. Semi-permanent, aboveground hooches were situated all over the hill, along with temporary hooches made from one or more ponchos snapped together. Sandbags were stacked everywhere.

Laying claim to LZ Jack was 5th Battalion's forward headquarters and tactical operations center (TOC). Of the battalion's five companies, four were rifle. Alpha, Bravo, Charlie, and Delta companies conducted search and destroy missions off base (brigade preferred the sanitized term search and *clear*, but it never really took hold). Each of the four rifle companies rotated from the field to LZ Jack to provide perimeter defense and to rest and refit. Echo was battalion's heavy weapons company. It remained on the LZ to provide cannon and mortar support to rifle companies in the field.

After touchdown, I toted my gear past a wooden sign that read:

WELCOME
TO
LZ JACK
GARRY OWEN

Originally an Irish drinking song from the eighteenth century, Garry Owen was adopted by the U.S. 7th Cavalry Regiment as the official marching tune in 1867. In the years that followed, the name became part of the regimental crest.

I had little difficulty recognizing the TOC. It had an assortment of antennas on its sandbagged roof, including a tall, omni-directional FM aerial supported by guy wires. I stepped down into the partially underground earthen room and reported to the operations officer of major rank who was expecting me. Alpha Company was currently operating in the field, he said, and I could expect to fly out in the morning to join them. *Swell.* In less than twenty-four hours, I would likely have a radio on my back humping the bush in the company of about 165 nomadic headhunters.

I made a point of telling the major about my military background and was pleased to see he looked somewhat impressed. But when I exaggerated the personnel officer's assurance that my time in field would be no more than two months, the major corrected me with a knowing smile. He said my MOS and prior training would indeed be a factor in securing a battalion radio job slot, but that I also had competition. Two other O5Bs had recently come to the 5th and both had worked at a radio school. They were currently in the field serving in different companies and, like me, would be vying for battalion radio job slots as they became available. When I asked for their names, he couldn't recall them. The officer dismissed me with instructions to remain within shouting distance.

I left the bunker and prepped a spot outside the entrance where I had the rest of the day to take in my environs. The camp had a discernable air of casualness about it; if there was a dress code, I didn't recognize it. Shirtless enlisted men didn't salute officers and officers didn't harass enlisted men with pointless, time-wasting duties. Life as a grunt was surely hard enough. I kept thinking about my competition, wondering if one of them was Eldon Smith, my friend and fellow classroom instructor at Fort Huachuca. He would have been my greatest competitor, but Eldon had received orders for Nam a few days after me, which likely eliminated him from the pool of candidates. Whatever credentials these radiomen brought to battalion, they had at least one advantage over me: both were already in the field gaining experience. I had to force myself to stop thinking about them and focus on what I could control. Ultimately, my company commander held the key to my getting out of the field. He was the one man I needed to impress most. Of course, all the men of Alpha Company were important. They too would have to accept me, and so I vowed not to let anything stand in the way.

That evening, I struck up a conversation with a seasoned grunt who was in from the field. I asked him to confirm the structure of a Cav rifle company and if it differed from others. He said his company's strength varied, but that it generally hovered between 140 and 165 men, including the command post (CP). Each company had four platoons—three rifle and one mortar—of around thirty-nine men in each. Finally, each platoon had three squads of about twelve men each.

When I told him I was a new radio operator flying out to Alpha Company in the morning, he said he could tell by my pack-rat tendencies. He warned me to shed all unnecessary weight from my ruck, claiming any cherry humping heavy in the bush for two weeks, and especially an unconditioned cherry lugging a radio, would quickly learn the hard way. "Dump the bulky air mattress," he said, "and the flak jacket."

"No flak jacket?" I asked in surprise.

"It's heavy and traps heat. Leave it. Besides, it don't stop bullets, only shrapnel." Somehow, that last comment didn't support his argument.

I asked him how grunts could live in the jungle for up to two weeks with only the bare necessities. He said helicopters called log birds dropped in supplies (code word *cigars*) when conditions permitted, but that I could expect to wear the same fatigues for several days at a time. Boxer shorts were superfluous in the field, so few men wore them. As for socks, he said, take two extra pair—one as a spare to help keep my feet dry (no better advice given) and the other pair to hold cans of C-rations. He preferred that method to storing cans in his pants pockets, which could lead to rashes on long humps. He told me to smash and bury any discarded cans in the field so as to deny nourishment to the enemy (and here I thought we destroyed them to conform to the Geneva Convention against the use of germ warfare). A better meal option in the field, though rarely available at that time, was the "lurp." Named after long-range reconnaissance patrols (LRRPs), lurps were freeze-dried foods packaged in single-serve plastic bags. To prepare, one need only mix in hot water. Finally, companies in the field were occasionally treated to "hots." Freshly prepared at LZ Jack, hots were foods kept warm in metal containers and delivered by helicopter.

My mentor ended by demonstrating how to pack a ruck properly to help keep important stuff dry, or as he put it, less wet. I dutifully followed his advice, with one exception. In spite of its bulk, the air mattress was coming along.

Before he left, I had to ask him how much fighting companies in the field were experiencing. He couldn't remember any recent campaigns, only that most enemy contacts were limited to small run-ins and booby traps. His company continued to discover enemy bunker complexes. Some were old and some showed signs of recent use. That led him to think Charlie was avoiding head-to-head contact with the mighty 1st Cav. If true, that was fine by me.

Below is a string of battalion daily reports that run from 8 September to 10 September, two days before my arrival in Alpha Company. Although I was not with Alpha at the time of these reports, I include them for two reasons. First, they provide colorful examples of what occurred in the field. Second, a significant number of daily reports, written during my time in company, were missing from the division's archives in Suitland, Maryland, where I did research after the war. An archivist there told me not all records made it to the archive, while others disappeared through theft.

By way of explanation, a Kit Carson is an enemy defector, or chieu hoi, a term to mean "open arms" in the Republic of Vietnam (RVN) amnesty program. Letters and numbers such as A 3/6 (or 3-6) are unit identifications and will be explained in greater detail later, as will code words such as *sub oak*. Referenced are two soldiers from 3rd platoon who received wounds by their own grenades. They may have sustained their injuries throwing grenades into enemy bunkers. "Frag it, then check it" was generally our policy before anyone descended into the bunkers. Line 1 is code for killed, line 2 is code for wounded. I include brackets for clarification.

8 Sep 68
1615H
A [Company] found trail with new foot prints. splits into W and NW. markings on tree were:

        NDA
        B

Kit Carson says it means hooch B this way. much remains there. he feels it was 3 day rest stop used 3-7 days ago.
1735H
A 3/6 contact with 2 gooks. no confirmed.
1810H
A 3/6 in pursuit.
1815H
A 3/6 found AK 47, found grid and sign on tree with drawing of trail network. below letter VA. kit carson says it means "caution, booby trap on trail."

9 Sep 68
0214H
A 1/1 reports movement NE. 4/6 to their SE. also a smell.
0835H
A checked area of last nights voice - neg.
0906H
A 3/6 finds one bunker cooking area used in last 2 days.
1055H

A 3/6 found 4 bunkers, jumped one gook, found blood spot. request tracker [dog team] (was neg @1142H).
1155H
A has Bailey Bridge.
1430H
A 3/6 found bunker area. found SKS, med. morphine, pen, ammo, det cord, food, diaries from officers etc. bunkers were 12x6x5.
1640H
A has 2 line 2's 3/6 leg and eye wounds from friendly frags. 1 only medevac.
1445H
A1/6 finds food, uniforms, blankets, medical.
1600H
weather wind gusts 20k 77° - 99°.

10 Sep 68
1600H
LZ Jack weather warning. fog-thunderstorms.
0715H
A 2/6 moving NW. A co moving SE.
0715H
A 3/2 suboak back to FOB with Chieu Hoi. was found going through garbage.
0950H
he is 24, from Hanoi. is in the infantry 1 Z unit. one of four battalions around Hue.
has SKS pack, 8 rounds ammo. approx 500 meters N of FOB.
1055H
Chieu Hoi could be a Captain or Dai Vy. says he is from 1st Div. 3rd Bn Z co - 3rd Bn.
has been moving to Hue from Hanoi for one year.
1417H
A 3/6 finds one grave marked:
       NC: Mihn Thu
       10-11-66
1645H
A 2/6 finds 3 bunkers, 1 hooch, 2 piles fresh waste.
1938H
A finds 1 hooch 10x4, 45 chicom grenades.

It is now early morning on 12 September, and the air is already thick as soup. Fog partially obscures the sun breaking over the horizon. A single Huey slick sits on the helipad at LZ Jack. Inside the aircraft, crewmen prepare for takeoff. Also inside, a few large plastic jugs of water…and one lone passenger loaded down in full gear. As the engine begins to whine, the large rotor blades begin to spin overhead, chopping the air slowly at first: whoomp— whoomp—whoomp. Faster: whoomp–whoomp–whoomp. Faster: whoompwhoompwhoomp. The helicopter teeters side to side as it begins to lift. Skids up. We're airborne.

Minutes later, the slick approaches a lush, forested mountain-side. I glimpse colored marking smoke mixing with fog within a small opening in the trees.

The drop zone.

Movement appears inside the clearing. A soldier. One of ours. The slick descends through the rising fog and hovers more than a meter above ground. One of the door gunners—the crew chief—hand signals for me to get out. I get off the bench, negotiate around the water jugs, and stand at the door. The angle of the terrain makes a landing impossible, but a little closer to the ground seems within reason.

"Out!" shouts the crew chief. His voice is barely audible over the noise of the whirling blades. The slick hovers no closer. I quickly assess the situation. Jumping from a standing position at this distance while wearing a heavy ruck would hurt like hell, or worse.

"Sit down and jump!" the crew chief yells. "Now!"

I comply and sit at the edge of the door with my legs hanging out, feeling for the landing skid with my feet. *Where's the damn skid?!*

Unaware of any better option, I push away from the aircraft, but not far enough. The ruck clips either the floorboard or the skid and I come down hard on my feet at an awkward angle. Gravity sends me sprawling to the ground. Quickly rolling to my knees, I avoid the water drop but not the embarrassment of a clumsy grand entrance. Flying debris blinds me. One jug bursts on impact, spraying me with water. Immediately after the final jug hits the ground, the Huey pulls up, dips its nose, and whisks off into the swirling, colored fog, leaving me in its backwash.

So much for a good first impression.

Company RTO

By the time I got to my feet, soldiers were busy collecting water jugs and showing little interest in their new cherry. I caught someone's attention and asked where to report. He pointed. "That'd be Captain Talbott," he said.

I walked toward my new commanding officer (CO) while sizing him up. He was tall and thin and looked to be in his late twenties. Stitched to the front of his camouflage cloth helmet cover were two black bars as his only visible rank insignia. Slung over a shoulder was a CAR-15 carbine rifle pointed toward the ground. His thigh pockets were bulging with plastic maps and such, and a pen was sticking out of a breast pocket. Beyond that, nothing really distinguished him from anyone else.

I stood in front of my new boss and saluted, but before I could report, Captain Talbott quickly pulled down my arm. "Don't salute in the field," he corrected me in a calm, even voice. "You never know who might be watching."

My day was starting out really well.

With arms at my sides, I announced, "Specialist Hoffmann reporting, sir."

The captain's narrow lips frowned on his narrow face. "Specializing in what?" he wanted to know.

"O5B2H radio operator *instructor*, sir."

His face took on a pained look as he proclaimed a need for riflemen, not radio instructors. I wholeheartedly agreed with his assessment, hoping he might put me on the next chopper out. As I recall, I may have even suggested it. But we all knew that wasn't going to happen. Like it or not, he got a radio operator and I got an infantry rifle company. The only thing left to decide on was my assignment.

To help influence his decision to keep me as his personal radioman, I gave him a synopsis of my military background. When finished, the CO's expression further deteriorated. He motioned to his executive officer (XO), and the three of us slipped away for a private talk.

When we were alone, Captain Talbott explained how my credentials put him in a difficult position. With few exceptions, RTOs within his company were 11 Bravo infantrymen who volunteered to carry a radio. I thought, *really? What the hell happened to all the O5B graduates from my radio school? Most of them get cushy desk jobs?* He went on to say how infantrymen new to the job honed their radio skills at one of twelve squad-level positions, each led by a sergeant. RTOs who demonstrated proficiency at squad level might later assume one of only four platoon RTO positions, with each platoon led by a lieutenant. Finally, the four platoon RTOs would be in the running to move up to one of the captain's two personal RTOs in his command post. That lengthy process helped to ensure competent, battlefield-tested veterans worthy of the captain's confidence and trust at the CP level. Both his RTOs had proven their competency under fire, and the CO didn't like the idea of demoting one of them for an untested cherry, even if that cherry had the rank and qualifications to be his personal RTO.

He considered out loud a more appealing option. Maybe he would send me to one of his four platoon lieutenants and let that officer decide what to do with me. Appealing to him, maybe. The way I saw it, any platoon leader would feel the same as the captain, and because shit runs downhill in the Army, some hapless squad leader sergeant would end up with an overqualified and unwelcome RTO, or an under qualified foot soldier without a radio.

While the captain was leaning toward the platoon idea, I was definitely leaning toward the CP. Under no circumstances did I want to end up in a twelve-man rifle squad, so I quickly made a request. I asked him to let me prove myself as his RTO, and in the unlikely event I failed to meet his expectations, I would expect a demotion.

Captain Talbott thought a moment. "I'll let you know in the morning. Now, let's saddle up."

My first day in the field could have gone a little better. Actually, it could have gone a lot better. On the positive side, we didn't come under enemy fire, and the captain let me walk behind him and his two RTOs in the CP. On the flipside, heat and humidity were off the charts as our hump took us up and down steep, tangled terrain. My unconditioned body withered under full pack, even without the radio. By early afternoon, I felt weak and dizzy. I found that I had no choice but to devote my full attention to keeping pace and to concentrate on the ground for foot-tripping roots and vines. It was tough going, and by the end of the hump I was exhausted. My two canteens were empty and my fatigues were soaked from sweat. And the day ain't even over yet.

The four platoons went about their end-of-day routines with quiet precision. They designed a companywide defensive circle and set out trip flares and claymore mines. One or more squads were sent outside the perimeter to act as listening posts (LPs, code words *lima papa* or *slash*).

The CP set up near the center of our small perimeter. There was Captain Talbott and his two RTOs, the XO, the company first sergeant (top), the head medic, the forward observer (FO), and the FO's radio operator. And one currently jobless cherry. Corporal Jablonski (Ski) operated the company radio. Corporal Potter handled the company's battalion radio. Both men propped their rucks up against the same tree to keep the radios together.

Captain Talbott told Ski to begin teaching me radio call signs and code words unique to the battalion and company. Ski dutifully followed orders, loathe he was to give aid and comfort to his possible replacement. He listed the most often used call signs, beginning with battalion at LZ Jack.

Fifth Battalion: Fast Flanker
Commanding officer (LTC Stockton): Fast Flanker 6
Battalion RTOs: Fast Flanker 6-5 (pronounced six-five)

Alpha Company: County Line
Commanding officer (Talbott): County Line 6
XO: County Line 5
Top: County Line 6 mike
Company RTO's Potter and Ski: County Line 6 India

First Platoon leader: 1-6
First Platoon RTO: 1-6 India
First Platoon's three squad RTOs: 1-1, 1-2, 1-3 (same for squad leaders)

Second Platoon: Same as 1st Platoon, but substitute a 2 for the first 1s

Third Platoon: Substitute 3s

Fourth Platoon: Substitute 4s

Call signs were often shortened during communications. Fast Flanker became Flanker and County Line became Line.

Ski added more call signs to my list before throwing in some code words, such as *oak* for a platoon and *sub-oak* for a squad. The full list was daunting in that I may need to memorize all of them in a very short time. Fortunately, some usage was already familiar to me, although all call signs and many code words were unique.

The forward observer's call sign was scarlet guidon 70 (pronounced seven-zero). He acted as liaison between our company in the field and rear artillery (arty) batteries (code word *redleg*). Part of his duties included verifying our unit positions and calculating defensive targets (DTs, code words *delta tangos*). This evening, I watched our forward observer prepare DTs while he referred to his topographical maps. First he estimated our position by using reference points (RPs) within a map grid, and did so utilizing the four major compass directions. He put the points into code using the same signal operating instructions (SOI) booklet all RTOs carried in the field. The booklet provided daily authentication tables we used to scramble and unscramble grid points to prevent an eavesdropping enemy from learning our whereabouts.

Because we were under heavy jungle canopy on this day, he instructed redleg at LZ Jack to load four harmless smoke rounds. They were set to airburst at each of the four compass reference points to help verify our position. After the distant cannons at Jack fired, the four shells exploded in the air over their respective compass points, sending out tentacles of smoke for easy viewing.

Our FO found his calculations were off target, but that was likely due to our maps; they were not always spot-on accurate. After recalculating, he tried again and received better results. Now if in the middle of the night the enemy attacked us, the FO could quickly call in a fire mission requesting a delta tango alpha (north), or delta tango bravo (east), etc., and adjust as necessary.

Sometimes our FO had to prepare delta tangos after dark when smoke rounds were difficult to see. Under those conditions, he would call in airbursts (ground bursts if we were in the open) containing white phosphorous (WP, code words, *whiskey papa* or *willy-peter*), which burned brightly in the dark.

On this night, after our DTs were established and our position was verified, Corporal Potter relayed our position to battalion in code. About the same time, Ski picked up the company handset and called the four platoons for a *penny count*, penny being code for an individual soldier. Each platoon was responsible for an accurate accounting of all its pennies at the end of each day to make sure no one was missing from the day's hump. Also known as foxhole counts, each platoon RTO coded his penny count before sending it over the air. Ski requested a penny count by issuing a niner-niner, which was a general call to all units on a given frequency, in this case, the platoons on Alpha Company's frequency.

"County Line niner-niner, Line 6-India, penny count, over."

Platoons always answered niner-niners in numerical order, starting with 1st Platoon.

"1-6 India, base plus twenty-nine, over."

Base was a predetermined number all RTOs knew in advance. In this scenario, base is ten. 1-6 India simply subtracted ten from his actual count of thirty-nine to come up with twenty-nine. Second through 4th Platoons followed in order with their own penny counts.

Dusk always comes early in the jungle. By the time light faded to dark, our night defensive position was set, LPs were out, and DTs were established. Foxholes were labor intensive, so soldiers manning the perimeter didn't always dig them, or at least not very deep. Those of us in the CP practically never dug them.

I cleared a piece of ground not far from the radios and put down a plastic ground cloth. I unfastened my bedding from the ruck, spread out the air mattress, and spent several dizzying minutes blowing it up. Doc may have been the only other person in the CP to have one. When finished, I watched some of the men fashion crude tents out of their ponchos, using sticks to hold them up. I copied their technique, spending a lot of time putting up my own crude mini-tent.

Sometime after chow, battalion's commanding officer at LZ Jack, Lieutenant Colonel Stockton, called his company commanders in the field to plan the next day's humps, as was his habit each night. Alpha Company was first up. When the call ended, Captain Talbott collected his four platoon leaders at our location to apprise them. The four officers (I believe they were all 2nd lieutenants at the time) took out their grease pencils and waterproof maps to mark the next day's routes before retiring to their sectors. Everyone then settled in for the night.

"Hoffmann, come here," Ski summoned in a hushed voice. I pulled on my boots and sat with him at the radios.

"You take first watch."

Damn, I forgot about nightly radio watch.

The problem with war is that it runs 24/7 with no time outs or days off. That's so uncivilized. How can soldiers be expected to kill and maim efficiently without adequate sleep? LBJ and Ho Chi Minh should have negotiated nights and weekends off for their fighting men. Maybe then a guy could get some rest.

Back to reality, the communists often moved under the cover of darkness when detection was less likely. They also were known to probe allied defenses after dark looking for weak spots. Demolition commandos, known as sappers, sometimes did the probing. Using stealth and patience, these half-naked specialists would carefully crawl their way through tripwires and other perimeter defenses carrying only explosive satchel charges. If they were lucky enough to breach the wire, they would run throughout the perimeter dropping their charges and then search for escape routes during all the confusion. Very likely, though, they would never make it in or out alive.

For security reasons, we had to monitor our radios at night. Command post personnel pulled two radio watches per night with each shift lasting about an hour. Much longer than that and a sleep-deprived foot soldier was apt to fall asleep at the switch. Watch fell to the captain's two RTOs, the FO's RTO, and the company medic. My entry into the mix meant we'd get some extra sleep. Ski's instructions were that I stay awake and remain quiet; keep the external speakers turned off; keep the squelch on and volume low to the handsets; rest the company handset on one shoulder and the battalion handset on the other so I could hear communications; request situation reports (sitreps) from all platoon RTOs and LPs thirty minutes after each hour; answer battalion's company-wide sitrep request, generally fifteen minutes before each hour; Alpha Company was always first to report; speak quietly into the mike; don't wake the next shift one minute early; and wake Ski and not the CO in case of a situation, although it better be dire. Last but not least, Ski told me to wake the next shift gently, because a startled GI can be deadly with his loaded rifle by his side.

Got it…I think.

I was familiar with the mechanics of sitreps, but that didn't relieve my nervousness about asking or giving one. It wasn't as though I had mike fright, but these conditions were different from when I led training exercises in the desert at Fort Huachuca. This was the real deal, with real consequences for screwing up. That's why I asked Ski to request the first round of sitreps in my presence as sort of a refresher. He reluctantly agreed. Everybody liked Ski and I understood why. He was an easygoing fellow willing to help others, even the cherry who might take his job.

When the time came to request a sitrep, Ski grabbed the company handset and squeezed the send button. He whispered, "County Line niner-niner, Line 6 India, sitreps, over." Each man on radio watch reported "Sitrep green," meaning he had nothing suspicious to report. LPs stationed outside the wire adhered to strict radio silence. Each reported green sitreps by pressing and releasing their send buttons twice, breaking squelch with each squeeze of the button.

Several minutes later, the battalion RTO at LZ Jack called over our battalion radio. "Fast Flanker niner-niner, Fast Flanker 6-5, sitreps, over." Alpha, Bravo, Charlie, Delta, and Echo Companies were to respond in that order. Ski picked up the battalion handset and whispered into it, "County Line 6 India, sitrep green, over." With that, Ski released the send button, gave me the handset, and disappeared into the dark.

Piece of cake, I said to myself. *Just as I used to teach it.*

Because both radios looked alike, with only their dials set to different frequencies, I had to be careful not to pick up the wrong handset. I placed the company handset on my right shoulder and the battalion handset on my left shoulder and rehearsed their positions. Then I leaned back against the tree and waited to initiate the next round of sitreps.

Except for innocent nocturnal animal sounds and buzzing mosquitoes, the jungle was fairly quiet. My fatigues were still damp with sweat and would likely stay that way overnight in the ever-present high humidity. No matter. Nothing was going to keep me from sleeping after my shift...well, other than maybe an enemy attack.

Enemy attack? What the hell am I doing here?

Another disturbing thought comes to mind: What if a trooper calls me with an immediate problem I can't handle? Probably make a bumbling fool of myself after declaring I'm a communications expert. Have to avoid that. Better to suck it up and wake Ski for the answer rather than risk screwing things up.

I checked the illuminating dial on my old Timex wristwatch. There was still plenty of time before making the call. Later, I looked again. Only a couple minutes had elapsed. *What's wrong with my damn watch?* I put it to my ear. It was still ticking, just like John Cameron Swayze promised in those TV ads. More time passed; my eyelids are getting heavy. I checked the time again. Finally, only minutes remained.

Near the appointed time, I picked up the company handset and counted down the remaining seconds, as if each tick mattered. After a deep breath and a moment's pause to practice the simple phrase, I squeezed the send key. "County Line niner-niner, County Line 6 India, sitreps, over." I spoke clearly but quietly into the handset.

Almost immediately, one radioman after another whispered his "green" reply, including those LPs that gave two squeezes of their send buttons.

"County Line niner-niner, County Line 6 India, roger, out." Great. Now all I had to do was to wait for battalion to call.

About a quarter to the hour, a voice broke squelch over Potter's battalion radio. "Fast Flanker niner-niner, Fast Flanker 6-5, sitreps, over," came the request. I was first in line and whispered into the second handset, "County Line 6 India, sitrep green, over." Other companies followed in their proper order.

"Flanker niner-niner, Flanker 6-5, roger, out."

Relief! My first watch ended without a hitch and I could finally get some sleep. But as I was about to make my way to wake the next shift, a calm voice broke squelch over the company radio, "6 India, how about a tango charlie, over?"

Uh-oh. The caller was asking for me, but I had no idea who he was and what he wanted. Tango charlie sounded like code words for something, either that or the guy thinks my name is Charlie and wants to dance. While I pondered what to do, the voice broke squelch again and made the same cryptic request. Because the call might be important, I couldn't continue to ignore it, but I also didn't want to wake Ski on a trivial matter. So what I did was swallow my pride and announce over the network that I was the new RTO and would the caller explain his request without breaking SOP (standard operating procedure). Otherwise, I would wake someone for the answer.

"Time check, cherry. All I want is the time. Maybe you should wake 6 and ask *him*."

I sheepishly provided the caller (and by extension everyone else on watch) with the time. Then I set out to find Ski with the help of a red lens flashlight. When at his side, I gently woke him for his shift and lied, saying everything went smoothly. From there I negotiated my way back to my air mattress. I took off my boots and damp socks to let my feet air dry, an essential routine for a foot soldier. From my helmet's elastic band I removed the insect repellent and doused all exposed skin to ward off malaria-carrying mosquitoes. The repellent kept bugs at bay, but its effectiveness would not last all night. Still clothed in damp fatigues, I covered myself with a poncho liner and laid my head awkwardly on the helmet.

The next dawn, I woke up scratching itchy bug bites and had a stiff neck from using the helmet as a pillow. For the next few nights, I tried laying my head on a rolled up poncho but got cheek rashes from it. I solved that problem by wrapping my dirty terrycloth towel around the poncho.

By the time we broke camp, my tango charlie incident had become the shot heard 'round the world. It seemed to me that most everyone was having a good laugh at my expense over something so trivial. I tried to deflect some of the sting by using self-deprecating humor, but inside I felt ridiculed by my peers. Surely I made too much out of it, but I was sensitive to how the men viewed me. Gaining their respect and avoiding similar pratfalls over the airwaves became paramount to me.

Fortunately, the silly episode didn't sway the captain from awarding me the position of company RTO. But as it turned out, I had little cause to celebrate. The announcement had an immediate and negative impact on many of the company's Skytroopers. They were none too happy to see some hotshot cherry radio operator take Ski's place at company level. Men in my position had to first earn that right, beginning at *squad* level. It was the way RTOs advanced in their line company.

Ski was hard to read after the decision came down, although he seemed to take the news in stride. For my part, I couldn't think of anything to say that wouldn't come across as disingenuous. Instead of talking to him then, I would wait until we were alone to bring up the touchy subject.

Before the order came to move out, Captain Talbott told me to follow behind Ski for another day or two without the radio. I was to monitor traffic on both company and battalion radios and finish memorizing call signs and code words. That was fine by me since I was in no hurry to lug the additional weight on my back.

By the end of the second day, it became painfully obvious that I needed much more time to absorb all the duties relating to the job. Learning conditions were less than ideal in the bush. By necessity I had to focus most of my energy on negotiating the terrain, maintaining the pace, and dealing with the withering heat and humidity. Oddly enough, getting into a firefight was the last thing on my mind. I was overly self-critical without recognizing that almost everyone around me was struggling to some degree. Even veterans of the bush were sucking wind, tripping, slipping, and snagging.

Troopers who didn't hurt themselves falling sometimes brought comic relief. The truly memorable tumbles were the head-first, equipment-spilling, "timmmberrr" varieties. Most falls occurred after fatigue set in when feet began to shuffle. By then, though, everyone was usually too tired to laugh.

That evening, I caught Ski alone and said I was sorry for the way things came down. He said all was okay. He understood why things happened the way they did, and he didn't blame me, the captain, or anyone else. Besides, he was near short-timer status. Ski let me off the hook, and for that he was aces.

Dawn of the third day and the jungle floor begins to morph into combinations of light and shadow. Smells of cigarette smoke and instant coffee waft throughout the perimeter. Troopers slowly move through the mist, pulling in their claymores and tripwires. Mortars are stowed and rucks repacked. LPs return to camp after radioing ahead so they are not mistaken for bad guys.

I woke up between my dew-covered poncho liner and flat air mattress. Apparently, I had overlooked a sharp object the night before when clearing the ground. I decided to send the mattress back on the next log bird and not ask for a new one, thereby forgoing one of life's little pleasures.

Troopers were cinching up their rucks when Captain Talbott turned to me and asked if I was ready to carry the company radio. *Hell no, I'm not ready!* "Yes, sir, ready if you are." It was the only answer to give. Though I had barely gotten through the past two days *without* the radio, any other response would have cast doubt on my stated abilities. Maybe I sold myself too well, but right now I needed to demonstrate confidence, not uncertainty.

The PRC-25 portable field radio, or "prick" as we called it, increased the weight on my body to eighty-plus pounds. Ski helped rearrange gear around my ruck to accommodate the radio, two spare batteries, and smoke grenades. Next, he gave me the codebook along with a warning that should I lose it, battalion would have to issue new codes and my name would be famous. As a result, I worried about that damn codebook for as long as it was in my possession.

With little difficulty, I slung the heavy ruck over one shoulder and inserted an arm through the shoulder strap. So far so good, but the challenge was yet to come. The weight and awkward angle of the ruck kept me from slipping my free arm through the second strap. Ski and Potter stood back watching my initiation with great amusement while I looked like a dog chasing its tail. When they finally took pity on me, Ski laid my ruck up against a tree and with the pack upright and square to the ground, he had me lean against it. Now I could easily slip the straps over both shoulders. Standing was another matter. For that, I rolled onto my hands and knees and then stood, lifting weight equivalent to a chubby fifth grader on my back. His work done, Ski bid the CP good-bye and disappeared to hook up with his platoon.

Captain Talbott told me to shadow him at all times and then gave the order to move out. That was my cue. I keyed up the handset and passed on his order, feeling the power of my words on a company of men.

Author

The CP occupied middle position along a single-file column of around 160 soldiers. After a couple minutes or so, the procession began moving out in front of me. Two of the three rifle platoons marched ahead of the CP. The third rifle platoon took rear position, or drag. All three rotated positions several times in the field, however, fourth platoon (mortar) usually marched immediately behind the CP.

Our company didn't always hump or camp together in the field. Platoons and squads often split out from the main body on separate patrols or functioned as defensive flanks. Leading any column was the point man, the most dangerous position in a rifle company. Point rotated from squad to squad within the assigned lead platoon. Most troopers dreaded the assignment, whereas a few sought the adrenaline rush. On this day, as with every day in the field, our point moved out with his M-16 held at the ready, locked and loaded on full automatic, safety off. His senses would be on high alert for any unusual sounds or smells. His eyes would probe the jungle in front of him for unnatural colors, structures, and movement. He would constantly scan the ground for tripwires and anti-personnel mines, and he would be acutely aware of his almost certain fate were he to walk into an enemy ambush.

We minimized idle chatter during the hump to maintain some degree of stealth. Potter had us turn off our speakers and clip our handsets high onto our shoulder straps to avoid missing incoming calls. That gave us one free hand while the other held our rifles. Few men shouldered their M-16s because in the jungle where visibility was often severely limited, you might need your weapon in a big hurry. Better to hold onto it for quick protection. Consequently, many soldiers discarded their rifle straps since they tended to get in the way.

When conditions allowed, we preferred setting our radios on squelch. Squelch cut out electronic noise, called "rush," an annoying *shhh* sound emitted from our speakers and/or handsets. Squelch also blocked out weak signals, a problem made worse when operating in dense jungle terrain. Unfortunately, most days we went squelch-less.

Conditions on the ground also determined which of two antennas we used. One was a ten-foot rigid mast. It had five, two-foot sections threaded together by an elastic cord. Each section slipped into the next to gain the greatest send/receive coverage, or they could be broken down and tied together. The other antenna was a one-piece, three-foot whip. It was flexible and resembled a stiff measuring tape.

Humping heavy took a toll on my already weakened body. Shoulder straps dug deep into flesh and muscle. I tried shifting the straps but experienced only short-term relief. By afternoon, it felt like hundreds of pins were jabbing my shoulders. Later in the hump, the pain became nearly intolerable when the pins turned into stabbing ice picks. It was only after I stuffed my terrycloth towel between the straps and my shoulders that I finally gained some relief.

I took an occasional call that morning, passing most questions and comments to the captain. At this point, I didn't know which calls he trusted me to handle, which calls I could delay, and which calls required his immediate attention. Until I got to know the Old Man better and learned what he considered to be routine and nonroutine traffic, I felt compelled to involve him. Captain Talbott must have expected the interruptions, but as the days wore on, he would show his annoyance. And Potter was of little help, which made me suspect he wished me to fail.

By late afternoon, I was in such ragged condition I could focus only on putting one foot in front of the other. Radio transmissions were little more than garble. "Get that, Hoffmann, it's yours," Potter would say repeatedly, finding he was listening to my horn as much as his own. "Pick it up," meaning the pace, was another oft-repeated line of his. The CO wasn't blind to it; he could see me struggling, too.

Somehow, I made it through the day, grateful to have come through the ordeal. That evening, the men in the CP seemed to avoid me, and who could blame them? Had we met the enemy that day, my slow responses on radio could have jeopardized lives. Without question, I had to quickly get into shape or risk losing my job and all credibility.

That night on watch (now two per night), I sat at the radios and sometimes shivered from exhaustion. I could expect about six hours of broken sleep every night, not enough to recharge my internal batteries in my weakened condition.

Sunrise came all too soon. Men around me began moving in their steady, purposeful ways while my aching muscles balked at instruction. I had just finished a morning C-ration and was in the middle of repacking when the order to saddle up caught me by surprise. All the men were throwing on their rucks while I scrambled around grabbing shit. "Move out!" the Old Man ordered. Still on the ground was my radio. I picked up the handset and relayed his order, and then resumed my packing. When the formation began moving out in front of me, I had barely finished cinching the pack's loose ends. I slung the ruck over my very tender shoulders and joined the procession.

My second day out in full gear began much as the first, except I had less energy and more muscle soreness. I made it through the morning, but only with great effort. By mid-afternoon, our hump turned up a steep and muddy incline, testing everyone's endurance. Sweat poured off me. My face throbbed in time with my rapid heart rate. My back and shoulders hurt terribly. My legs ached. I felt dizzy and sick to my stomach. The distance between the CO and me lengthened. And then the unthinkable happened.

On a particularly steep climb, my legs gave way and I collapsed to the ground, unable to get up. My body shut down, and I lay there struggling to get air into my oxygen-deprived lungs. Men behind me came to an abrupt halt (happily, I should think). Potter came forward, himself short of breath. He cajoled me to get up. When I did not, he grabbed my handset and ordered the formation to stop. Captain Talbott heard the commotion and descended the embankment, digging the heels of his boots into the dirt. He asked if I was hurt. I vaguely remember saying no, only that I was out of shape, having had little PT for almost a year.

The Old Man called up a hearty trooper who unstrapped the prick from my ruck and took it, along with my codebook. Another trooper grabbed my rifle. *What's going on?* I wondered as the CO took my handset and squeezed the send button.

"Move out," he ordered.

I looked up in horror. The captain starred back at me and growled, "Get your ass up and join the company, or sit there and rot, unless the gooks find you first." With that, he turned back up the mountain.

I remained on the ground in near panic at the thought of being abandoned. *Surely he's bluffing. It would be criminal to leave me here.*

Whatever the captain's intention, this was not the time or place to test his resolve. Minus my radio, my rifle, and my dignity, I found the strength to stand on shaky legs and rejoin the procession, able somehow to push on.

So let's see: I'd been with Alpha Company for a grand total of four days, and with little effort managed a public relations disaster. I could not have made a worse impression on my captain and the rest of the Skytroopers, even if I had scripted it.

That evening, I approached the Old Man and apologized for my physical breakdown. It was easy; I had no pride left to swallow. I wanted my radio back and promised a better performance the next day, as if I knew something nobody else did. The captain nixed the radio request, but softened his stance. He said he didn't like hearing excuses from his men and was pleased not to hear any now. In war, he said, only results mattered. This was not a game, and there were no awards for second place. Everyone struggled in the bush and everyone suffered in the bush, but we did so together in support of one another.

I came away from the meeting with a new understanding of what the captain expected of his men: work together to survive. Unless a trooper required medical attention in the field, he would do his job. Period.

Ski returned to the CP and temporarily took back the radio while I once again took up position behind him. For the next few days, our company continued humping slippery slopes through dense jungle, and I continued to struggle even without the extra weight on my shoulders. Near the end of our stint in the field, Captain Talbott returned my radio. This time, he didn't ask if I wanted it, although my answer would have been the same as before.

Plagued by extreme fatigue, I persevered through our last couple of days in the field. My senses had dulled, which led me to make several dumb radio mistakes. My self-confidence, once unshakable, collapsed along with my body on that mountainside. Still ringing in my ears was the commanding officer's threat that he would leave me to rot in the jungle.

When the day came for us to return to LZ Jack, I felt like a pummeled boxer saved by the bell. Within an hour of Potter making the call to battalion, a line of slicks arrived on station. "County Line 6 India, Sabre 1, your push (frequency), over," came the call from the lead pilot over our company frequency.

Potter listened while I answered the call in this manner: "Sabre 1, County Line 6 India, I read you lima charlie (loud and clear), over." I might also have said five by five, both being the upper limit on a sliding scale. The first five is volume (loud) and the second five is clarity (clear).

"6 India, Sabre 1, what's the condition of the papa zulu (pickup zone), over?" The pilot's voice was shaking from the vibration of the aircraft.

After checking with Potter, I said over the handset, "Sabre 1, Line 6 India, we have a two slick, cold papa zulu, over," meaning there was enough room to land two helicopters and that the company was not taking enemy fire.

"Roger 6 India, pop smoke."

Potter anticipated this point in the communication and had already removed a smoke grenade from his shoulder strap. He pulled the retaining pin and threw the canister inside the landing area. After an initial *pop*, colored smoke hissed from both ends of the can and billowed into the sky.

"Sabre 1, Line 6 India, smoke popped, over."

After a pause, the pilot responded, "6 India, Sabre 1, I identify red smoke, over."

"Sabre 1, Line 6 India, affirmative, red smoke, over."

"6 India, Sabre 1, coming in."

"Sabre 1, Line 6 India, roger, out."

Had I been the first to reveal the color, and had VC been in the area listening to our transmission over another radio, they could have popped the same color to lure the sortie into a trap.

Lead platoon's three squads gathered at the tree line as the first two slicks descended onto the PZ (PZ was used interchangeably with LZ). Helicopter door gunners lowered the barrels of their M-60 machine guns upon entry but continued scanning the tree line for enemy muzzle flashes. Depending on the number of slicks in a sortie, several sorties might extract a company. The CP was among the first group out; that way the captain could coordinate activities at the next LZ. When our turn came to board, the Old Man held me aside to let others board ahead of us. Those who couldn't fit on the single canvas bench seat had to either squat or sit on the metal deck. Captain Talbott took a spot at one end of the bench and yelled over the noise for me to sit at the edge of the deck with my legs dangling out. I complied, but my heart wasn't in it. He motioned with his hand that I bring the handset to my ear and monitor company transmissions. Signal strength would be stronger with my antenna near the open door.

As the chopper lifted, I leaned back and grabbed onto anything tied down with my one free hand. Once over the treetops, the slick nosed down and accelerated until it reached greater knot speed before ascending. I felt a tad unsteady at the open door, but coped until the aircraft abruptly banked my direction forcing me closer to the edge. I dropped my handset. At the same time I felt a hand grasp my ruck. It wasn't a dangerous situation; it just caught me off guard. Probably caught the captain off guard as well, for he instinctively grabbed my ruck instead of nudging both it and me out the door, thus solving his RTO problems. Of course I say this in jest...he wouldn't have wanted to lose his radio and codebook.

I would be involved in numerous airlifts as an RTO, and my seating position was often the same. Luckily, I didn't suffer from vertigo or a fear of flying. After a few similar flights sitting at the edge, I actually got accustomed to living on the edge.

When our sortie reached LZ Jack, another rifle company—the one we were replacing—waited to fly out on the same slicks. Once we had boots on the ground, platoons fanned out to their appropriate sectors where defensive bunkers and slit trenches dotted the perimeter. Troopers had the option to sleep in bunkers, but they generally avoided entering the damp, rat-prone fortifications. More often, troopers built temporary aboveground hooches. They would collect several ponchos, snap them together, and hold them up with vertical sticks, or hooch poles. Depending on the number of ponchos used, several troopers could cram under them.

The company CP bunker was located farther inside the perimeter. Built partially aboveground, its roof was made of corrugated metal covered with sandbags. Sand-filled ammo boxes and more sandbags further reinforced the short outside walls. A nearby generator provided electricity to the radios, one ceiling light bulb, and a small oscillating fan. The CP bunker was large enough to accommodate the captain, the executive officer, the first sergeant, and the commo (radios), but not the radiomen. Potter and I had to find separate accommodations adjacent to the CP.

My hooch was a metal culvert half. It looked like an elongated igloo about seven feet long, four feet wide, and only three feet high. It was set up on a row of ammo boxes and covered by a single layer of sandbags. Ponchos hung over the two open ends. Less than a week earlier, I would have considered these digs uninhabitable. Today, it was more like a room at the Holiday Inn. It even came with an air mattress.

I crawled into the tight space through the front flap, stowed my gear, and had just fallen asleep on the mattress when the flap swung open.

"Got room for one more?"

Hell no. "Gee, I don't know, it's pretty cramped in here."

"Move over a bit and we should be able to fit in another air mattress."

And with that, I had a roommate.

Steve Meche hailed from some Louisiana backwater and had a thick bayou accent to prove it. He was short and stocky, but not fat (few in the field carried around extra body weight, at least not for long). Our two bodies and gear made for a tight squeeze, but we managed all right and managed a friendship as well.

For the next three or four days, I looked forward to a few simple pleasures, like resting my worn-out body, writing letters home, and eating hot meals with an occasional scoop of ice cream. I concentrated on putting to memory all the code and slang unique to this company, and worked damage control to my public image. Somehow

I had to prove to everyone that I was a regular guy in spite of my poor performance in the field.

One afternoon I forced myself to walk the perimeter and meet some of the men. I thought if they could see and talk to the man behind those erratic transmissions, they might cut me some slack. It was a fantasy of hope. Most troopers showed little interest in talking to their captain's new RTO, and those that did were generally blunt with their comments: "So, how is it you got the Old Man's radio right off?" And, "If you're such a hotshot horn, how come you're fuckin' up?" And, "You're going to get somebody killed if you keep fuckin' up."

From their words and tone, one might think I was carrying an enemy AK-47, wearing black pajamas and sandals. Now there's a thought. Think of all the attention I would have gotten then. I saw little advantage in trying to gain favor from men unwilling to give it, so I retreated to my hooch, feeling rejected by my peers.

If ever I needed a letter from home, it was now. Mom promised to write often, as she always did when I was far from home. For my part, I had been writing family and friends whenever possible, but after nearly a month in country, I had received precious few letters, and all were old postmarked. When they finally did catch up to me in Alpha Company, they did so in multiples, and most were from Mom.

She was the kind of mother who would worry herself sick if she knew I was in a rifle company, so I led her and Dad to believe I worked at Camp Evans and away from most dangers. But like all mothers, she still worried about her son.

In a letter to a friend's mother, dated 27 September 1968, she expressed her concern:

> Dear Eunice,
>
> ...Phil is near the northern part of South Vietnam in the mountainous part and is in a new camp. They are living in tents and in his off duty he spends his time being a carpenter building the buildings they need. Poor Phil! My heart aches for him. He says,

however, he is fine and that he hasn't seen anything of fighting except for helicopters overhead being on alert. I shudder every time I think of him sleeping in those darn tents when it is raining. He says it feels like the Boy Scouts and wishes it really was....

Dorothy

I told my brothers and a few friends about my actual job, and asked them not to tell my parents. The deception worked for a while until someone at home slipped up. Even then, no one really knew what I was going through. How could they without experiencing it?

Near sunset each evening, one or more squads or half squads, called teams, walked off LZ Jack to pre-established points on a map to act as listening posts. Once in place, LPs had to be careful not to compromise their positions. Troopers had to remain quiet and maintain strict radio silence. They were not to build hooches or use illumination, which meant no smoking or cookfires. It was lousy duty no one wanted, particularly on stormy nights. For that reason alone, squads or teams sometimes feigned leaving the perimeter and instead hid out in camp.

Daytime reconnaissance was also a standard procedure at Jack. On this particular morning, Captain Talbott ordered two squads to fly out on a day's recon a few klicks away. Leading the unit was their platoon sergeant, Staff Sergeant Reynolds, who had his Skytroopers hump light.

The Old Man and I were alone in the CP bunker when Sergeant Reynolds called from the field. He reported they had boots on the ground and that his two sub-oaks were moving in separate directions. I acknowledged his call and watched the Old Man exit the bunker.

A few minutes later, Sergeant Reynolds began yelling over my external speaker, "Contact! Contact!" And then, "Do you read me, over? Do you read me, over?" He was expecting a reply without first releasing his send button. Yes, I could hear him and the small-arms fire in the background, but I couldn't respond to his message until he released his damn send button. Making matters worse, the other squad's RTO was trying to transmit at the same time and that was causing transmission bleed-over. Now all I was getting was garbled noise. Until they stopped "stepping" on each other and both let up on their buttons, I would just have to wait.

From the bunker's entrance, I summoned the captain and hurried back to the radio in time to discover the net had cleared. I keyed the handset, "Line 3-6 mike, Line 6 India, be advised: release your send button when finished speaking. Wait one for six." Just then, Captain Talbott and others entered the bunker. I gave them a quick report before the CO told me to alert battalion while he dealt with Sergeant Reynolds. I complied.

Getting a detailed sitrep from the veteran sergeant proved no easy task while he was in the middle of a chaotic firefight. Complicating our communications was his irritating habit of holding down the send button between transmissions. At some point, we were able to learn that his men had run into a VC force of about equal strength. Captain Talbott remained composed, telling the sergeant to estimate his position in the clear so we could quickly call in support. Next, he turned and ordered me to immediately alert redleg of an upcoming fire mission and then request helicopter gunships from battalion. His orders were crystal clear. Less clear was how I was going to perform them. My stateside training had not covered procedural alerts for fire missions and requests for gunships. That was usually the forward observer's job, but the FO wasn't in the bunker. However, the XO was present and he noticed my indecision. He took over the battalion handset and made the requests while I sat there feeling mostly inadequate.

The firefight was intense but short-lived. Afterwards, one medevac picked up the few casualties and took them to Camp Evans, while additional slicks extracted everyone else back to LZ Jack. We waited near the helipad to greet the sullen troopers, who only wanted to return to their hooches after they landed. Sergeant Reynolds wasn't so lucky. He had to report to battalion TOC and provide an afteraction report. Casualty numbers were low.

On our walk back to the CP bunker, the empty slicks flew overhead on their way to Camp Evans. When they got to the other side of the LZ, one of the helicopter door gunners fired a stream of bullets from his M-60 machine gun. We hurried back to the radios, where Captain Talbott called the lead pilot and required an explanation. The pilot said his door gunner spotted a deer and killed it. The CO blew his stack. Yelling over the handset, he berated the pilot, telling him how friendlies could have been in the area on recon. That drew an apology, but Talbott was unappeased and reported the incident to battalion.

Once again, the Old Man took me aside for a little talk, and this time I expected the pink slip. Instead, he assigned me no blame for not knowing how to perform his earlier directives. He did, however, stress how he had the entire company to think about and not just one individual. Regardless, he was giving me a little more time to get up to speed.

But not much more.

The strain of the last several days probably lowered my resistance to a point that I developed a splitting headache, fever, and chills. After finding someone to assume my radio watch, I bundled up inside my little hooch and popped aspirin. In the middle of the night, I woke up in a sweat and laid my arms on top of the poncho liner, being careful not to disturb Steve, who was sleeping to my right.

Sometime before dawn, I felt a mild tugging sensation on the middle finger of my left hand and thought I was hallucinating. But then, as my head began to clear, I opened my eyes in the dark and instinctively jerked my left arm. That's when I heard a loud squeak and saw a large, cat-sized shadow leap up, flip around in midair, and scurry out the front flap.

I screamed and sat up, crashing my throbbing head against the metal culvert before falling back, barely conscious. My scream startled Meche awake. He screamed at my scream and grabbed his sixteen.

"What?!" he yelled as he prepared to blast away.

I came to my senses in time to yell back, "Don't fire! Something bit my finger."

Steve put down his rifle and reached for a flashlight while I told him how a rat the size of a tomcat tried to make a meal of my hand, starting with the tip of my middle finger. He examined the finger and found the skin red but unbroken, which meant I wouldn't have to go through a series of painful rabies shots. Next, he checked my head and found a goose egg, but no blood.

We spent some time securing the bottom of our hooch flaps, and then covered ourselves completely with our poncho liners. For the remainder of the night, I drifted in and out of sleep listening for scratching or gnawing sounds. Fortunately, Ben the rat didn't return, and by morning my high fever broke.

Top's tour of duty had come to an end, and while he waited for a chopper at the helipad, a group of us gathered to see him off. Top was about to take the short ride to Camp Evans before catching a flight to An Khe where his stateside clothing issue was stored. From there, he would go to Cam Ranh Bay where a "freedom bird" would fly him and others out of Southeast Asia and back to the "real world." With little fanfare, Top climbed aboard a Huey and flashed us a smile. When the skids lifted, we gave him a thumbs up and he responded in kind as the helicopter whisked him away.

Until a new first sergeant reported to Alpha Company, Captain Talbott temporarily promoted our ranking E6 platoon sergeant to the position of top. He was none other than Staff Sergeant Reynolds, the platoon leader involved in the earlier contact. Over the next several days, the bulldog-faced, crew cut, career soldier proved less in command of the job than was his predecessor. On the positive side, he was less demanding, which suited me fine.

Alpha Company had been at LZ Jack for probably four days when the Old Man announced we were flying back to the field in the morning. The mountains were once again our destination, in an area where intelligence had reported enemy movement.

Intelligence could have come from a variety of sources, such as aerial reconnaissance, enemy interrogations, electronic listening devices, and ground units like ours. Elite, long-range reconnaissance patrols (lurps) also provided intelligence. Lurps—named after those freeze-dried food packets—operated in small groups of generally four to six men. Their missions in the field were to document signs of the enemy, and to do so with stealth. Because of their small numbers, they generally avoided enemy engagement unless, of course, their cover was blown. To avoid compromising their locations, helicopter resupply was not always possible. Sometimes, a lack of supplies forced lurps to live off the land during their many days in the bush, something their training prepared them to do.

The thought of conducting another two-week operation in the mountains worried me. I had shed too much weight in too short a time for my body to properly adjust. Already my watchband hung loosely around my wrist. I had to push the band up my forearm where sweat would prevent it from slipping. To help keep my body sufficiently hydrated in the field, I clipped an additional half-gallon water bladder onto the utility belt.

When conducting operations in the field, a foot soldier's fatigues were most often damp from sweat or soaked from rain. Few troopers ever bothered throwing on ponchos during brief daytime showers because after the rain stopped, body heat dried them back to damp. Steam would actually emanate from them. Ponchos were uncomfortable to wear, anyway, and they held in moisture. So we typically wore them during all-day soakers or end-of-day downpours, when the chance of evaporation was unlikely.

Humping in damp fatigues never really bothered me; that very dampness helped to cool my skin under the tropical sun. *Sleeping* in damp fatigues was another matter. During my first trip into the bush when my core body temperature was out of whack, I would sometimes lay shivering on the ground at night. To have had something dry to wear over my upper body would have been helpful. But then keeping anything dry in the bush was nearly impossible. Empty ammo cans served as good watertight storage units, but they also added weight and bulk. I used small sheets of plastic to keep stuff dry and experienced poor results. My camera was covered in some, but condensation rusted the lens shutter, anyway.

There really were only two areas on my person to keep anything dry. One was the space inside my helmet liner above the webbing. It was there I kept a handkerchief for my screwed-up sinuses, and letters and pictures from home. It was a good place for small things.

A less reliable dry spot was inside my rolled up poncho. There I kept extra socks and a cotton T-shirt. Yet, no matter how tight I cinched the poncho with bootlaces, water always found a way to seep in. And naturally, whenever I unrolled the poncho during a storm, those items were further exposed to the elements. The cotton T was useful when dry, except like most everything else, it didn't stay dry for long. And wet cotton didn't hold in body heat.

On my second trip out, I took someone's advice and packed a long-sleeve, woolen undershirt. Wet or dry, wool held in heat. It also felt scratchy to anyone with a wool allergy, which I happen to have. After a couple nights of intolerable itching, I had to pitch the wooly.

Before we flew back to the field, our company received boxes of free stuff called care packages. Among the items were dozens of paperback books and cartons of cigarettes. I rummaged through the boxes and picked out a book and a carton of Marlboros. I didn't smoke, and up to now I had ignored those little four-pack cigarettes included inside boxes of Cs. This time, I thought, why not grab a free carton and puff some cancer sticks to pass time?

I put the book in my ruck and lit a cig. It made me lightheaded and I snuffed it out after only a few puffs. A couple minutes later, I lit another and experienced the same result. Free or not, cigarette smoking held no appeal. Neither did the book; it remained in my pack.

A sortie approached our LZ carrying Skytroopers from a sister company rotating out of the field. After the slicks landed and grungy riflemen off-loaded, we rushed to the open doors, instinctively dipping our heads because of an irrational fear of decapitation. I took my customary position at the edge of the door with my legs dangling out. Rotor blades picked up rpm and dust. The lead ship commander gave notice to his fellow pilots for skids up. Soon, our fully loaded slick was ascending a few vertical meters before it nosed downhill to gain speed.

When our slick leveled off at altitude, the door gunners released their gun grips but kept vigil over the lush countryside scarred by bomb craters and defoliated trees. Gun batteries at LZ Jack were busy prepping the area around our insertion point. They fired salvos of high explosives (HE) to discourage bad guys from hanging around. As our string of slicks closed on the LZ, the lead pilot instructed redleg to cease fire. Moments later came the reply, "Tubes clear." A final round of WP exploded near the LZ, releasing its tentacles of white phosphorous into the air. That was our visual cue to advance.

Skytroopers on the first slick hit the ground running. Although they met no resistance, the LZ wasn't necessarily danger free. Charlie could still be bunkered within the tree line, lying in ambush until more Skytroopers exposed themselves. When everyone was safely on the ground, Captain Talbott marshaled his troops and gave the order to move out.

During the day, Alpha Company came across more than one interconnecting footpath used by the enemy. We examined them all to determine their age, width, signs of recent activity, and direction of travel. Potter forwarded our observations to battalion TOC for documentation and tactical planning.

Captain Talbott sent us up the most recently used path, but we failed to initiate contact by the end of day. The next day we met the same result.

On possibly the third day out, the squad leader on point called me with information about an intersecting path. They found several fresh sandal prints running into our path that continued ahead of us. His platoon leader called to say he was on his way up to see for himself.

While we stood in place waiting for the lieutenant to report, mind-dulling boredom instantly switched to heart-pumping alarm when automatic weapons fire erupted at the head of the column. Instinctively, everyone ducked off path. The lead RTO yelled over his radio, "Contact! Contact!" Captain Talbott grabbed my handset to get a sitrep just as the shooting stopped. "Let's go," he ordered, motioning to Potter and me to follow him up path.

On our way, the lieutenant gave a sitrep, saying he and his point man were conferring on path when approximately ten unsuspecting VC walked into view. His squad opened fire and the enemy fled without firing a shot. Some even dropped their weapons as they ran. The lieutenant wanted to give chase, but the CO denied the request. He instead ordered a team up path, but only a few meters to pick up discarded equipment and look for blood trails.

When we arrived on point, three VC were laying on the ground. Our soldiers had killed two and wounded one. I stood gawking at the VC and didn't notice Captain Talbott turn back down path. He and Potter were probably busy on the horn with battalion and didn't notice my absence.

Only a few squad men were present and watching Doc tend to the severely wounded VC. The young Asians were dressed in shorts and sandals and all looked terribly thin. I found it hard to believe they were soldiers. Without their AK-47s, they looked more like harmless teenage villagers.

The lieutenant claimed to have killed one of the dead and stood over the body gloating like a hunter after bagging a trophy buck. The VC was face down on the ground. Blood covered parts of his face, the result of taking a round to the head, I guessed.

Suddenly, the "dead" VC twitched. A thin smile grew on the young lieutenant's face. He looked down path. Satisfied the captain was out of sight, he raised his M-16 and flipped off the safety. He pointed the muzzle at the wounded VC, and while I looked on in disbelief, the lieutenant squeezed off four rounds into the soldier's back. Lowering his weapon, he slowly turned to his men as if looking for approval when he caught sight of me. His smile vanished. Staring directly at me, he said with emphasis, "The gook was going to die anyway." And then, in an unmistakably threatening tone, "You remember that, Horn."

I turned to see the CO's reaction and saw he wasn't in sight. Anticipating I might be in jeopardy, I nodded my head in agreement and hurried back down path only to meet Talbott and Potter on their way back up. The CO demanded to know what the shooting was about. Still reeling from the lieutenant's threat, I claimed ignorance. The captain took my handset and called the lieutenant, who gave some bogus excuse. Then the Old Man turned his attention to me. "Dammit, Hoffmann, don't leave my side." Potter looked contented.

Not knowing how the captain would react to the incident, I didn't correct the lieutenant's version of it. Instead, I waited for someone else to come forward. If the lieutenant had been outed—and he was not—the captain could have brought up serious misconduct charges against his junior officer, but only if he were so inclined. He could have also quietly given him a verbal reprimand, dismissing the incident because the enemy soldier was about to die anyway, which, in my opinion, he surely was. Or the CO could have ignored the sordid episode altogether. Again, I didn't know how the CO would react, but I did know this: if I had informed on the lieutenant, and had the captain done little or nothing about it, I believed the lieutenant would have exacted revenge. My life was complicated enough without having to worry about friendly fire.

In a letter I sent home to friend Ron McDaniel, I wrote:

> Do you sleep warm in your bed at night? We would except it's the monsoon season and most of the time we go to bed wet and get up wet. Did I say bed? I haven't been in a bed since I've been here. We make tents out of ponchos and sleep on the ground. If we don't sleep wet from the rain, we sleep wet from our own sweat. A shower...what's that? Get the picture Ron? I could go on and on.
>
> I'm stationed at Camp Evans, which is near the DMZ. My boss here said that he wanted me to learn how they use a radio in the field before I get a good job. That's where he put me. I'm humpin' a radio in the jungle on search and destroy missions. We eat, sleep and hump in the jungle. Believe me, I haven't had it so rough physically and mentally as I have here.
>
> One day we came into contact with 10 gooks (VC). We killed one, wounded two and the rest got away. A Lt. wounded a gook and then while the gook was lying helpless on the ground, he put four more bullets in his back. These guys love to kill. What the hell am I doing here?
>
> Well, have to sign off for now. I have to write Uncle Sam and tell him exactly what I think of him. I'll say, "Sam, you can take this funky-ass war and stick it up your McDaniel."

Battalion wanted us to follow the VC up path, but not until a Kit Carson flew in to help identify possible trail markings. When our chieu hoi finally took up position with lead platoon, the sun was getting low in the sky. Flanking squads split out to guard against ambush as the main force moved slowly up path. The blood trail eventually ended, but we still had fresh sandal prints to follow. By the end of the day, we had not initiated contact. The Old Man had us set up perimeter near path and left the flanking squads out. Throughout the night, all watches reported green sitreps.

The next morning our hunt resumed. Flanking squads occasionally had to hack their way through heavy underbrush with machetes. Sometime during the day, I got a call from our point man. Sandal prints appeared to veer off path, he said. About that same time, one of our flanks called to say they found a shallow grave, recently dug.

Captain Talbott ordered the grave unearthed and sent up the Kit Carson to inspect it. When the report came back, we learned that the grave contained the body of one VC recently killed from small-arms fire. Other than a half-clad corpse, there was no identification, weapons, equipment, or other markings at the gravesite.

We claimed a body count of one to battalion and then continued up path with our intrepid point man leading the way. No doubt he was concentrating fully on the task at hand, for he would get no do-over. The slightest mistake or lapse in concentration could easily cost him his life, and possibly the lives of men behind him. He was damn good at his job, but not infallible. On this day, our point man failed to detect a thin wire stretching across the path, ankle high above the ground.

BOOM. The sound was unmistakable. When the grenade exploded, small-arms fire did not follow, and that meant booby trap. Captain Talbott grabbed both handsets and raced up path, pulling Potter and me behind him like we were dogs on short, pig-tailed leashes. At the head of the column, we found the point man and another soldier lying on the ground grimacing in pain. Doc tended to the injured while Potter called for a medevac.

We hadn't had enough time to construct a PZ when the helicopter arrived. As a result, the medevac had to lower a litter basket through the trees. Each of the wounded was winched into the aircraft to receive additional first aid and a ride back to a medical facility. Both would live, but I think their injuries were million dollar, meaning they would be going home.

After the extraction, we located the source of the booby trap. Tied to a tree off trail was an empty C-ration can damaged by the explosion. Some careless GI probably discarded the can without first crushing it, and a Viet Cong guerilla made good use of it. The VC had tied it to the tree and slipped in a grenade after removing the delaying fuse and safety pin. The can prevented the grenade handle from springing open, which would have set off the device. A tripwire had been attached to the grenade and strung across the path and tied to another tree. When our point man tripped the wire, the grenade pulled out of the can, releasing the handle. With the delaying fuse removed...instant *kaboom*.

To get more bang for his buck, the VC could have run the tripwire parallel to the path a few meters before wrapping it around a tree and then across the path. That way, the blast would come from behind our point man, putting more GIs at risk.

Charlie employed an array of booby traps and other devices to use against us, from primitive punji sticks stuck pointy-side up at the bottom of camouflaged holes, to toe-popper land mines that had a nasty habit of separating one's foot from one's ankle.

Staff Sergeant Reynolds's promotion was short-lived. Alpha Company was still in the field when our new top sergeant choppered in to assume the duties of ranking NCO. First Sergeant Shaffer was a wiry military lifer who looked too old to be in the field humping a heavy ruck. At least I thought so. Aside from his large glasses that sat crooked on his nose, his wrinkled, weather-beaten face, gray whiskers, and buzz haircut aged him more than his forty-eight years. Captain Talbott naturally asked Sergeant Shaffer about his past military experience. We learned he had fought in World War II and Korea, and that he volunteered for a rifle company in Vietnam.

Top turned out to be a crusty, by-the-book career soldier who gave no quarter and asked none. Despite his gruff demeanor, it was impossible for me not to respect this remarkable veteran of three wars.

Hale though he was, Top labored under his ruck until our company descended into the foothills, where a gentler terrain eased some of the strain on all our bodies. For the next few days, we continued operations in the lower areas trying to make contact with an elusive enemy.

Late one morning, we stopped at the edge of a large clearing and called for pony express mail. Within the hour, a log bird honed in on my marking smoke and dropped a couple of bags before pulling away.

An easygoing trooper named Chamberlain stood ready to gather the bags that were lying about thirty meters into the clearing. I thought he could use some help and offered my assistance. We left our gear behind and waded through knee-high elephant grass to the drop point. Just as we picked up the bags and started back, a VC hiding in the opposite wood line opened fire on us with his AK-47.

Chamberlain and I immediately dropped our bags and sprinted for cover. I ran bent over, zigzagging through the grass. Bullets thudded into the ground. Fear turned my legs into rubber and I fell at least once. Troopers started putting out suppressive fire to our front. Now bullets were whizzing by us from opposite directions. That took the zig out of my zag. Chamberlain and I reached the tree line at about the same time and dove for cover. When all the shooting had ended, we looked at each other, panting heavily.

"You hit?"

"No. You?"

"No."

Smiles came to our faces. We made it! We goddamn made it!

The Old Man sent units around the wood line in both directions to find the VC who couldn't shoot straight. To no one's surprise, he disappeared without so much as a blood trail. Later, after everyone regrouped, less nervous volunteers fetched the bags.

Fifth Battalion got a new commanding officer by the name of Lieutenant Colonel John (Quickdraw) McGraw, and almost immediately he put his stamp on battalion. He exhorted his field captains to increase enemy body counts. "Get the gooks" was his mantra. He also demanded that every trooper wear a flak jacket in the field, whereas most men, at least in Alpha Company, shunned them. His directive didn't go over well, but the colonel was unswayed. He said all companies in the field could expect flak jackets on future log birds, and by God, every swinging dick would wear one. What's more, he wanted assurance from his field captains that all 5th Battalion troopers were digging foxholes every night in the field. He got the answer he wanted to hear, if not the results.

Captain Talbott passed the colonel's orders to his disgruntled lieutenants, who thought it was punitive bullshit. Predictably, the captain backed up his colonel, but he also predicted the new commander would reverse his decision over time on the jackets. As for digging foxholes every night, after a few nights of digging, the captain turned a blind eye and continued to let conditions on the ground dictate their necessity.

Soon, each trooper in Alpha Company was wearing a bulky flak jacket under his ruck, like it or not. Some men in the "not" category were so bitter over the colonel's directive that they began to "accidentally" lose their protective vests.

One morning toward the end of our rotation in the field, Lieutenant Colonel McGraw informed us that he was flying out in the afternoon. He wanted to inspect the troops and spend the night. We suspected he wanted to count foxholes and flak jackets and then find an excuse to leave. Captain Talbott told his platoon leaders to get their men squared away for our VIP visit scheduled for later in the day.

Sometime midafternoon, we stopped at a small LZ and took in water and bags of clean fatigues in advance of the colonel. Men picked through the laundered piles looking for anything close to fitting that wasn't new and stiff, and ignored the boxer shorts. Afterward, we cleaned our weapons for inspection and waited for the colonel to arrive.

Eventually, two choppers approached our position. The first was the command-and-control (C & C) helicopter carrying our battalion commander and others. The second was a log bird bringing in, to no one's surprise, hot food and ice cream. After the Hueys landed, the first to step out was the colonel. Behind him emerged one of his RTOs and an officer of major rank. A reception party of all company officers lined up and saluted when the colonel approached.

Lieutenant Colonel McGraw was a gangly man with slightly hunched shoulders, shaved head, and pouty lips. The oval shape of his head reminded me of the Grinch character in a Dr. Seuss book. He looked all business, and I thought if he gave more than a slight smile his face would crack.

Following the formal introductions, we saddled up to gain distance from our compromised location. After a short hump, we stopped to set up a night defensive position. Troopers went about their nightly routines, including the not-so-routine digging of foxholes. Captain Talbott sent out additional LPs to increase security, and our FO scrutinized DTs with redleg.

As expected, Lieutenant Colonel McGraw conducted inspection. He walked the perimeter, going from one foxhole to another asking those typical colonel-to-his-troops questions like, "What's your name, son?" and, "Where you from, son?" Occasionally he got off script: "Where's your flak jacket, trooper?" Our unhappy camper ended up spending the night after all and fussed over a number of issues with the captain, not the least of which was the mystery of the lost flak jackets.

Over chow, I got to know the colonel's radioman, Digger. He was a tall, good-looking New Yorker who had a pleasant demeanor and broad smile. I told him about my stateside background and mentioned battalion's offer to bring me up after two months in the field. Digger looked surprised. He thought the earliest opening for a new battalion RTO was in December. Given that scenario, my time humping the boonies would double to four months—not at all a pleasant thought. I wondered now if I would ever get out of the field.

The next morning, I boldly introduced myself to the colonel so he might remember my face and name. Indelibly, I hoped. He received my advance openly, and I took advantage of the time. I told him I was his future radio operator temporarily assigned to the field. "I look forward to being your RTO real soon, sir." "Good," he said. And with that he turned his attention elsewhere.

Good was good. A little weak maybe, but still good. Better would have been, "Well, Specialist Hoffmann, why don't you jump aboard my command ship and ride back with me now."

Only in my dreams.

Two days before our extraction back to LZ Jack, a large storm front rolled in and stalled over us. Massive thunderclouds turned the sky to black. Lightning bolts flashed and thunder clapped unnervingly close to our position. Probably the loudest rain I had ever heard poured through the triple-canopied jungle.

All RTOs tied clear plastic over their handsets to keep them dry. Throughout the night, everyone wore ponchos over their rain-soaked fatigues to hold in body heat. Sleep proved difficult at best.

After sunrise, the rain was still falling and the sky was unusually dark. Only by looking at my wristwatch and smelling cigarette smoke did I know it was time for another morning routine of eat, crap, pack, hump, hunt. Ponchos would stay on all day. Captain Talbott sent 2nd Platoon out on a separate course from the company with the understanding we would hook up later that afternoon. To help maintain commo with all units, RTOs affixed their tall mast antennas. All morning long, troopers slipped and tripped along sloppy, uneven jungle terrain.

Sometime that afternoon, our point man turned down a particularly steep ridgeline. The distance between each man widened as everyone dug his heels into the slippery mud while grabbing underbrush or anything else for stability. More than once, our column had to stop after a trooper took a header.

I carefully negotiated the slope at a safe distance behind the captain to avoid bringing any more attention to myself than I already had. Potter, unfortunately, was not as careful. He was walking close behind me when he tripped and fell forward. Before I could dodge impact, Potter propelled me down the slope feet first...directly toward the Old Man. Captain Talbott had only time enough to turn and accept his fate. He looked like a skier facing an avalanche in the instant before I took his legs out from under him. Men below us scrambled out of our way as we tumbled down the muddy slope before coming to an abrupt stop against underbrush. We lay there in a heap, ponchos up around our necks and covered in mud. The Old Man was pissed off, and I caught the brunt of his wrath. It didn't matter that Potter initiated the fall. Oh, no. It wasn't Potter who tripped him—I did.

That night I slept in my mud-caked fatigues, but I wasn't alone. That same afternoon, a flash flood washed several troopers from 2nd Platoon down a ravine. No one was seriously hurt, as I recall, although some equipment was lost.

Only a light rain was falling when a line of slicks arrived in the morning to pluck our company out of the field. They came to take us back to LZ Jack where I could get a proper shower, change into dry fatigues, and get out of the damn rain.

By the end of my second trip out, I had dropped approximately twenty-five pounds, down to about 135. It was a fair estimate without benefit of a scale, because my body compared favorably to when I was a gymnast in high school at about the same weight. The good news was that my body had finally adjusted to the rapid weight loss, and as a result, my stamina and endurance had returned. Taken together, I found I could concentrate on radio operations and avoid stupid mistakes.

Back at Jack, Steve Meche and I noticed that whoever recently vacated our little culvert hooch had dug a shallow trench around the outside of it to channel running water away from man and materiel. The trench did its job; we remained relatively dry throughout the night, even when the rain picked up in intensity.

I woke up thinking it was the middle of the night and checked my watch. It was actually after sunrise. I carefully shook Steve awake and told him we should get something to eat. He said we should wait until morning. Boy, did I have news for him.

I hunched over my air mattress and peeked out the front flap to notice the rain coming down pretty hard. The sky was dark, and a thick fog enveloped the area. Under these conditions, I felt sure battalion cooks weren't flipping eggs under an open-sided mess tent. Steve wasn't so sure. Never one to miss a hot meal, he struggled putting on his boots and poncho, and crawled out the flap. Before long, he was back inside our cubbyhole carrying only a long face. Guess it was going to be one of those C-ration and instant coffee kind of days.

Squad RTO

When my early morning radio shift came up, all I had to do was put on my boots, poncho, helmet, and grab my sixteen. After a quick trip to the latrine, I traipsed through the mud to the CP and followed trickling water down the steps into the damp bunker. The CO, the XO, Top, and Potter were there, along with an unknown trooper sitting in the corner. I offered hellos and had just taken off my poncho when Captain Talbott said he needed to speak to me. The look on his face telegraphed bad news. Coming right to the point, he said I hadn't progressed fast enough as his RTO and that he found a replacement. The hardness and brevity of his statement caught me flatfooted. I'm thinking why? Why after all this time and steady improvement does he decide to drop the hammer now? Up until our last trip into the field, I worried about just such moment. But in the last two weeks, I had performed well.

Hard as it was for me to admit, I acknowledged our talking about this very possibility. But I also claimed to have made adequate progress at the position. Captain Talbott disagreed. Without explanation, he said he was sending me to Lieutenant Fakler's 1st Platoon and that the lieutenant would assign me to one of his three squads. *Wait a second. What's that?*

"Squad, sir? Not platoon?"

Captain Talbott thought it would be best for everyone. *Maybe for everyone else*, I wanted to say.

So that was it. Me, this one-time hotshot radio instructor demoted to a twelve-man rifle squad, the lowest radio position in a rifle company...hell, probably the whole United States Armed Forces. The Old Man said Lieutenant Fakler was expecting me the following

morning. In the meantime, he wanted me to fulfill my morning shift
and answer any questions my replacement might have.

Potter's shift was at an end, and as he threw on his poncho
to escape through the exit, the stranger in the corner pulled up a
chair next to mine at the radios. His name was Corporal Gilmore—
Lieutenant Fakler's former RTO and my replacement. The moment
was awkward. It reminded me of when I took Ski's job, except my
role had reversed.

Gilmore spent the morning cozying up to the officers and Top
and all but ignored me. I assumed he had no questions until Potter
made a brief appearance. Then he had some, and all were for Potter.
Apparently, talking to a demoted RTO was beneath him.

Mercifully, the Old Man ended my shift early. As I prepared to
leave, Top told me to vacate my hooch. Swell. I lose my job and my
sleeping quarters all in the same morning. Gilmore and I exchanged
directions. His hooch was near 1ˢᵗ Platoon. I told him my hooch was
out the door to the left.

Before I left the bunker, Captain Talbott took on a conciliatory
tone. He said that after I gained more experience, he would have me
back at the CP. Sincere or not, these were words I needed to hear,
because at that moment I felt like a rock climber hanging onto a
ledge by his fingertips without the benefit of a lifeline.

Steve was still inside our hooch when I entered and gave him
the news. He tried to sound supportive, but no amount of encouragement could have helped me at that moment. I thanked him as we
parted company, not knowing if we would ever see each other again.
As it turned out, we didn't. Not long afterwards, Steve came down
with malaria and left the company, never to return.

I searched for Gilmore's hooch through fog and rain while trying
to figure out what led to my pink slip so late in the game. Other than
a minor screw-up or two our last time out, not including that muddy
tumble that was not my fault, I thought my performance passed
muster. Somebody influenced the captain. But who? Certainly
not the platoon leaders; they had synergy with their own RTOs.
Not the XO. We got along fine, and besides, he was aware of my

improvement. The only other person with enough clout to sway the CO was our new first sergeant. Top humped with the CP and could see and hear almost everything I did. What he could not have known was my progress at the position, new as he was to the company. He probably graded everybody, and he didn't give A's for effort. Maybe it was Top, or maybe not, but right now none of that mattered. I had to get over my hurt feelings and focus on Lieutenant Fakler and my soon-to-be squad sergeant.

Gilmore's hooch sat isolated on the side of a hill, looking like a lost rowboat at sea. Why he chose that location away from his platoon I didn't know, nor did I particularly care. For me at that moment, it was a perfect spot since I wasn't feeling very sociable anyway.

The small hooch was only slightly more substantial than what troopers fashioned in the bush. I found a poncho stretched over a horizontal cross-brace supported at each end by to two vertical sticks. Gilmore had staked the sides at an outward angle, giving the hooch an inverted V pup tent look. The poncho's hooded head hole was at the top of the cross-brace and tied off with a bootlace.

I crawled in and sat on Gilmore's inflated air mattress. After struggling to remove my poncho, ruck, and boots, I wiped the mattress dry and laid back, knees up to keep my stocking feet under roof.

I stared up at the poncho's knotted hood and contemplated my miserable lot in life when something about it caught my eye. A droplet of water was forming at the sphincter. As it swelled in size, the weight of the droplet increased until the force of gravity caused it to break free. My eyes tried to follow the bead of water to my stomach...*plop*. I looked up again to see another droplet form...swell... *plop*. And so it went.

The diversion amused me, so I made a game of it, trying to guess the precise moment at which the next drop would fall. To keep my shirt from getting too wet, I put my hand on my stomach at the point of impact. The time between each drip was somewhat evenly spaced: drip...drip...drip. I got good at the guessing game until, like all games, I tired of it, at which point my concentration focused from the ceiling to my hand. The relentless dripping had suddenly gone from amusing to annoying and then to downright uncomfortable. Eventually it became unbearable, like some kind of bizarre Chinese water torture designed to break me. I removed my hand and covered my stomach with a piece of plastic. That didn't help. The monotonous plop...plop...plop noise against plastic was more than I could bear. *Make it stop!* I pulled on my boots and crawled into the rain to tie a second knot around the head hole using a spare bootlace. Then I scampered back inside and waited anxiously for the results. Success! The dripping stopped.

About that time, rain increased to cats-and-dogs intensity. More water came rushing downhill, up and over the grooves of the air mattress wetting the length of my back. I slid off the mattress and further inflated the ballasts, but found the tactic mostly ineffective. Any time I moved, rivulets of chilly water ran down the mattress channels along my torso. Only by raising my shoulders slightly and remaining motionless could I avoid getting soaked. The position, however, was impossible to hold for very long. Eventually I gave up trying and let the water run its course.

It was at that moment life lost all meaning to me. I felt utterly alone stuck in that wretched hooch. Helpless, hopeless, and rejected, I succumbed to despair and cried uncontrollably.

Sleep did mercifully intervene, if only for a short time. When I awoke early that afternoon, reality drove me back into despair. Conditions outside and inside my hooch had not changed appreciably. For the longest time I lay frozen in place, staring through tear-glazed eyes.

Either by chance or by fate, I remembered the book packed somewhere inside my ruck. I reached in and pulled out Hemingway's *The Old Man and the Sea*, hoping that by reading it my thoughts would travel to a better place.

Of all the books I could have chosen, *The Old Man and the Sea* turned out to be a remarkable tonic for all that ailed me (actually, the fact that I had chosen a book at all was remarkable). I instantly identified with the story's protagonist, an old Cuban fisherman named Santiago who, while fishing alone at sea in his small boat, hooks a great marlin. The valuable fish is so big and powerful that it pulls Santiago and his small boat perilously out to sea. Instead of cutting the line and returning safely to land, Santiago refuses to give up and instead vows to battle the great fish to the bitter end. His exhausting struggle against impossible odds is eventually rewarded, if only temporarily. With his torn, bloodied hands, Santiago lashes his prize to the boat and labors toward shore, only to lose his worthy adversary to other forces of nature.

I found myself engrossed by the old man's extreme adversity. Many times his weathered body seemed beaten, and yet he persevered through a myriad of obstacles, eventually making his way back to land. Santiago's tenacity and unyielding will to survive inspired me. After finishing the short book before dark, my situation felt less dire. I began to cope, having survived my own rough waters that day with the help of an old fisherman and two of the book's quotes: "Keep your head clear and know how to suffer like a man" and "A man is not made for defeat. A man can be destroyed but not defeated." I put the book down on my damp chest, crossed my hands over it, and slept.

There was no joy in Mudville the next morning, except to say the main weather front finally pushed through. It left behind only a drizzling rain shrouded in fog. I wrested my gear from the small quarters, dismantled the hooch, and repositioned it to higher, more level ground. After a change into dry clothes and a visit to the mess, I slogged to 1st Platoon and reported to Lieutenant Fakler. The curly blond-headed 2nd lieutenant's perfunctory greeting demonstrated a lack of interest in the captain's unpopular, former radioman. Standing next to the lieutenant was Staff Sergeant Carter, the mustachioed E6 platoon sergeant. He was easy to read by his dour look and crossed arms.

I dutifully listened to LT (lieutenant) outline my responsibilities as squad RTO. They were less involved than my previous position, which I suppose was the whole point of my demotion. Everything was going smoothly, right up until he overemphasized the importance of properly handling radio traffic. I knew what he was getting at, and I would likely have bowed to his criticism but for the words of Santiago: A man can be destroyed but not defeated.

Raising my voice in opposition, I interrupted the officer and told him my past mistakes and lapses in concentration were due to exhaustion from being out of shape. I stressed that I was now physically fit and therefore able to concentrate on my duties. The lieutenant let me vent without censure before issuing a challenge. He said that if I performed well during our next trip into the bush, he would consider promoting me to his platoon RTO. Sergeant Carter looked pained at the very thought of it.

Lieutenant Fakler summoned Sergeant Larson, the squad leader of 3rd Squad. After a quick introduction, the buck sergeant led me to his defensive sector at the perimeter. Along the way, he gave me a quick rundown of the men in his squad (maybe twelve in all), including his second-in-command team leader. Sergeant Larson advised me to be careful around the edgy short-timer, who was none too happy I had come to their squad.

We stopped at a perimeter bunker, where I exchanged pleasant hellos with two men. Behind the bunker, small makeshift hooches of various shapes dotted the area. One of the largest was only a roof made from several ponchos snapped together and supported by hooch poles. Several men from 3rd Squad were huddled under it, along with two from another squad, about six (the team leader was not among them). All the troopers were smoking cigarettes and telling stories while music from the Armed Forces Radio Network played in the background over a transistor radio.

Sergeant Larson and I squatted at the edge of the hooch where he introduced me to an apathetic group of grunts. He suggested I get to know them better and then abruptly left me in the lurch. I remained squatted, waiting uncomfortably for an invitation to join their conversation, but none was forthcoming. Stung by their neglect, I fought off an urge to escape back to my crappy hooch and invited myself in. I was that determined to upgrade my reputation with these Skytroopers. A couple guys actually scooted over, albeit reluctantly. I removed my wet poncho and ducked inside, trying to be careful not to get their overlapping ground cloths any muddier than they already were.

The men resumed their conversation with nary a look in my direction. I tried to ignore their slight by forcing a happy face. I nodded my head at their stories and manufactured laughs whenever they laughed, all to gain their attention. When that didn't work, I tried something more proactive. At one point, I slipped in a couple of innocuous words, like "I agree," and got more attention than I had bargained for.

The mood in the hooch turned on a dime. Coming to mind was that classic scene from so many old westerns: You'd be a'knowin' it, by gum. It be the one where the outta town cowpoke done enter through the saloon's swingin' doors, and 'fore the doors stop a'swingin' the piany player stops a'playin', and the rowdy crowd stops a'jawin', and all heads turn to stare at the stranger as if his pecker is a'hangin' out 'tween his chaps. Yep, that be the scene.

Now that I had their undivided attention, I presented my case, in much the same way as I had with Lieutenant Fakler. When finished, I made a simple request of the men to give me another chance. While a couple guys looked mollified, the others saw my hardship claim as a crutch. They made it clear to me that all cherry soldiers faced added hardships in the field, including when they were cherries. But they still had done *their* jobs. I avoided the temptation to contrast my situation with theirs, for to do so would have only increased tensions. So I kept my emotions in check and simply told them things were different now that I was in shape. Most of them looked unconvinced.

This was a tough crowd to reason with, and the hardest among them to influence was Tex, the aptly named Texan from 2nd Platoon with whom most others joined sides. Another guy, Davy Miller, didn't pile on, and if anybody had a reason to be sore it was Davy, for it was his radio I was taking. Davy cut me slack, as did Flip Throckmorten, probably Davy's best buddy. This didn't mean we became friends. Their alliances still remained with their infantry-trained ilk.

After the mud settled and tensions eased a bit, my relationship with the men hadn't improved all that much. Still, they had heard my case and seen me in human form, not as some phantom radio voice. Gaining acceptance would take time, maybe a lot of time, and only after I proved competent at my job. I eventually left their cramped quarters and returned to my lonely hooch feeling emotionally exhausted. It had been an especially tough two days.

Along with the job came a new call sign: 1-3—1st Platoon's 3rd Squad RTO. Naturally, the lower position came with fewer responsibilities than my previous role as company RTO, but it was not without pressure. I had new procedures to learn, new personalities to impress, and psychological beatings to overcome.

My initiation began before nightfall along LZ Jack's perimeter. A squad member showed me field-of-fire angles from our bunker to minimize overlapping firepower with adjacent bunkers. He showed me how to detonate claymores and under what circumstances to do so. If I detected movement in the wire on night watch (now only one shift per night), my instructions were to alert the squad and report the situation to the company RTO. If a trip flare went off in the wire, I was not to assume it was due to an enemy probe and begin blasting away. Acquire a target, he said. More likely, a nocturnal animal would trip a flare. No one showed me how to load and fire the M-60 machine gun, and I never bothered to ask.

In the middle of the night, Davy woke me to pull watch. He accompanied me back to the trench to answer any questions. At one point, he noticed the illuminant dial on my wristwatch and urged me to either flip the watch face over or pocket it. That way, gooks couldn't spot the light and draw a bead on me. Well, before you could say Speidel Twist-O-Flex, I flipped over my watch.

After Davy left, I leaned up against the wall and trained my eyes along the perimeter looking for any sinister movement. The combination of partial moonlight and broken clouds cast eerie shadows along our defenses. The mere idea of a sapper slinking through the wire with lethal intent gave me the willies, however low the odds. Anyway, everything I might need was at arm's length: M-16 locked and loaded, additional magazines at the ready; claymore detonating clickers all in a row; a box of grenades; a flare gun with illumination rounds; a poised M-60 machine gun; a prick set on squelch, speaker off, volume to the handset.

Toward the end of shift, my tired eyes settled hypnotically on a shadow along the defenses. I stared dumbly at the same spot when something jolted my senses into full alert. *Something's moving outside the wire!*

I stared more intently. *No, it's nothing....*

No, wait. I bore in on the ghostly image.

Movement again. My heart rate and breathing increased.

Quick, put out the alert. No, not yet. I had to be absolutely sure not to send out a false alarm.

My eyes hurt from focusing on the object. *Oh, shit!* The once nebulous shadow took on a faint human form.

"Gooks in the wire!" I whispered.

Slowly and deliberately, I raised my M-16. At the same time, I turned my head to locate the radio handset. With one index finger poised at the trigger and the other poised at the send button, I looked back to discover only a benign shadow. *What the?* I relaxed my fingers and refocused on the spot, squinting like someone trying to make out the smallest letters on an eye chart. Once again, the shadow took on human form. I blinked a couple of times. Again, it changed.

It was then I knew what was happening. I lowered my guard and sighed in relief, remembering the first time my eyes had played a trick on me. I was a child at the time, lying in bed one Easter eve, waiting to catch the Easter bunny hide colored eggs. "Don't you wait up," Mom warned me, and only me, as she kissed her three boys goodnight. "He'll only come if you're asleep." I considered her words but decided to stay awake and not include my older brothers in the plan. Middle brother would only tell on me, anyway.

I sat up in bed listening for unusual sounds in the house and never took my eyes off the darkened doorway lest bunny appear. Santa, the tooth fairy, and the Easter bunny had always avoided me in the past, but tonight would be different. Tonight was mine. All I needed to do was stay awake and alert.

Eventually, my patience paid off. Something moved at the doorway. Bunny! A very tall, shadowy bunny was sitting up on his hind legs. He remained at the doorway until I averted my eyes. Then he disappeared. But not for long. He came back; he always came back.

Bunny didn't speak, but I spoke to him until Mom turned on the bedroom light and scared him away. Mom gave me a scolding and said what I saw wasn't the Easter bunny, but my eyes playing a trick on me in the dark. She turned out the light, and over my protest, shut the door. At the time, I didn't understand what she meant about eyes playing tricks, only that she and bunny were in cahoots.

Trying to catch all my elusive benefactors in the act went on for more years than I'm comfortable admitting. I think the year the jolly old elf was outed was the same year he gave me a Remington electric shaver and a bottle of Old Spice aftershave.

After that night on perimeter, I quietly performed my duties keeping mostly to myself. Radio communications within 3rd Squad were light, and they would remain so until Alpha Company airlifted back into the mountains. When the day came to mobilize at the helipad, Skytroopers packed heavy with one notable exception. Colonel McGraw let the "every swinging dick must wear a flak jacket" order quietly fade away.

I performed well in the role of squad RTO in the field. I felt less stress and quickly adjusted to the squad's procedures. As a result, Sergeant Larson found no reason to criticize my performance which I took as a rare pat on the back.

One day our company came across a path showing signs of recent use. We followed it cautiously until it met a connecting path, also recently used. Captain Talbott split off 1st Platoon down the less-used path while the rest of the company continued on the other. Lieutenant Fakler ordered 3rd Squad to take the lead, which put me in fifth position behind our point man. One or two positions behind me was the team leader, who groused about LT assigning our squad to the front. Right away he demanded I stuff the flexible, three-foot whip antenna down my shirt to limit me (and by extension him) as a target. He knew a priority of the enemy was to knock out communication, and our commo was located on my back. I complied with his directive but made the mistake of telling him our signal strength would suffer. In no uncertain words he told me never to question him again.

Sometime that afternoon, point found sandal prints going at a right angle off path. Sergeant Larson radioed, "1-6, 1-3, over," and apprised Lieutenant Fakler of the situation. Our squad received orders to follow the sandal prints, but only for a few meters. Point cautiously led our twelve-man unit off path. With each step the jungle closed in around us, further obscuring our view. VC could be hiding anywhere in ambush, if that was their intent.

Each of us held our weapon at the ready, locked and loaded, safety off. No one dared speak, including our anxious short-timer. Whatever level of stress he was under, the seasoned warhorse was still highly skilled at his position. For now, at least, I welcomed him at my back.

The sound of small-arms fire in the distance stopped us dead in our tracks. The company RTO called to say they surprised a small group of VC on path and opened up on them. The VC immediately broke contact. While the company waited for a medevac, our squad continued ahead until we came upon a shallow grave, recently dug. It was now clear: we had been following a burial detail.

Sergeant Larson relayed the news and received the anticipated order to dig it up. Graves, whether fresh or old, were usually unearthed to gather evidence, such as the number of bodies, cause of death, and any documents and insignia. Naturally, when our squad sergeant asked for a couple of volunteers, nobody in his right mind stepped forward. To break the impasse, he invoked the Army's most time-honored tiebreaker, loosely defined as shit runs downhill. And so the grave-digging went to his two newest men, one of whom was me. The rest of the squad, clearly enjoying our undertaking, retraced their tracks several meters to avoid the predictable smell.

Once they were out of view, my baby-faced fellow gravedigger stepped back and told me to start digging. Apparently he was under the illusion he was to supervise. I corrected him, saying Sergeant

Larson ordered *us* to dig up the grave. Thus began our give and take. He said he'd been with the squad longer. I complimented his achievement. He wanted to know how long I'd been in the Army, as if time in service had some bearing on seniority. I told him I was serving in the Fifth Army stateside while he was still taking classes in high school. It was now my turn. I asked him his rank.

"Private first class," he said.

"Specialist fourth class. Start digging."

"Don't pull rank on me." He was right, of course. Rank meant diddlysquat under these circumstances. Sergeant Larson ordered both of us to dig, and if we didn't start digging, and soon, the sergeant was certain to return, chew our asses out, and we'd still have to dig. Putting our differences aside, we found common ground on the following points:

1. The contents of the grave would provide no useful evidence.

2. The sight and smell of it would make us puke.

3. We would lie our titties off.

My co-conspirator and I used entrenching tools to overturn a thin layer of dirt on the grave. Then we hiked back to the squad and reported our disappointing find. We said that after an exhaustive search, we had found one partially decomposed male gook in shorts with no visible signs of trauma and no documentation. Fortunately for us, our cover-up worked, and Alpha Company added another dead VC to its confirmed body count.

Third Squad made it back to 1st Platoon, but 1st Platoon wasn't able to connect with the company before dark. Captain Talbott ordered us to set up a night defensive position and said we would hook up in the morning.

After the perimeter was up and everyone had settled back for chow, our team leader paced the area in a state of agitation. He predicted the enemy would attack our lone platoon overnight, and he demanded that everyone remain sharp until a slick plucked *him* out of the jungle for home. He ranted on about the men he knew who were killed within the last thirty days of their tours, and by God that wasn't going to happen to him. [There was a common story in the bush that grunts were more likely to be killed during the first or last thirty days of their tour.]

No one dared speak or look at the short-timer while he rabbited on. "Where's Horn," he yelled, turning in a circle until he spotted me. I pretended not to hear him. With fire in his eyes he walked up to where I sat, bent over me, stuck his finger in my face and threatened, "If you put me or this platoon in danger, Horn, I'll kill you myself." With that, he stomped away.

I continued to eat while pretending to everyone watching that his threat didn't bother me, but inside I was shaking. This veteran soldier of many campaigns clearly had the capacity to kill, and in light of his current mental state, I knew his was no idle threat. Now twice threatened by my own men—the first being the veiled threat from the lieutenant who shot the gook in the back—I began to think I had enemy on both sides of the wire.

Fortunately, we had a quiet night, outside and *inside* the wire. The next morning, 1st Platoon hooked up with the rest of the company.

It may have been the same day when our company's point man came upon an abandoned spider hole. Platoons fanned out and everyone inched forward. Troopers began discovering more abandoned spider holes, and then a bunker. A soldier fragged it. No bodies were inside. We kept advancing until we reached a complex system of bunkers nestled among the trees. The bunkers had to be cleared and checked, and so riflemen went about the job. I watched Flip remove a grenade from his shoulder strap, and while troopers aimed their rifles at the entrance to a bunker, he pulled the pin and tossed in the grenade. Men near the entrance immediately moved away and covered their ears. A few seconds later, dirt and smoke belched from the opening. After the dust settled, Flip searched the bunker with a flashlight. It was empty. We had similar results with all other bunkers.

The deserted compound proved to be a way station and storage depot. We discovered a sizeable cache of rice with individual portions still smoldering over warm embers. We also found medical supplies and a weapons cache, all abandoned during the enemy's hasty retreat. Battalion flew in choppers to collect the assets before our company continued maneuvers.

Alpha Company remained in the field several more days, but I have only two other recollections of that time. Our team leader had served his tour of duty and was going home. As his chopper lifted him away, troopers gave him the traditional thumbs up. I played along, but it wasn't my thumb I wanted to extend. My other memory is that of a bad case of jungle rot I developed on my neck. Under several days' growth of whiskers, itchy scabs spread from my chin to Adam's apple and from ear to ear. Doc gave me some kind of ointment and said to keep the area clean and shaven, as if sanitation in the bush were even possible. It took all the courage I could muster to put a razor to my soapy neck. Not only did each run of the blade lop off whiskers, each run sliced off smelly, bleeding scabs. Afterward, my oozing, mottled neck looked like a third-degree burn. The guys couldn't help but notice and began calling me leper. But after several days of painful shaving and ointment applications, I lost the jungle rot and, thankfully, the nickname.

When slicks brought us back to LZ Jack, I immediately shed my grungy fatigues and jumped under a crude makeshift shower. It was something I looked forward to doing each of the next three or four days on camp. I also planned to frequently check in with Lieutenant Fakler so he wouldn't forget about his future radioman. Other than that, all I wanted to do was rest, write letters and sleep. War, however, got in the way.

One night, the Viet Cong probed a nearby LZ, possibly looking for a soft spot in advance of an all-out ground attack. As a precaution, LZ Jack went on heightened perimeter alert. We shifted to a two-man, two-shift schedule. Naturally, troopers bitched about the extra shift and less sleep. It also didn't help that our booming howitzers at Jack were firing H & I at all hours of the night.

Newly available to us on perimeter defense was an allocation of starlight scopes. We had one in our bunker. At night, my fellow watchman and I took turns looking through the instrument that resembled a telescope. Its internal workings amplified ambient light, turning black landscape into a greenish hue. This amazing technology helped us distinguish between benign shadows and something far more sinister.

The following afternoon Lieutenant Fakler ordered 1st Platoon to pack light and meet ASAP at the helipad for a combat air assault. I passed his order on to 3rd Squad and then stripped my ruck of all non-essential gear for the one-day mission.

Arty was busy firing salvos in response to a fire mission while our platoon gathered at the PZ. A line of slicks was waiting there for us; their rotor blades were chopping the air in slow rotations. Lieutenant Fakler quickly briefed us on the mission. He said a lurp team on recon had blown their cover to an enemy force of greater strength. The lurps were able to withdraw to higher ground atop a crude LZ, but they were currently pinned down and taking heavy fire. Our orders were to fly in, reinforce the patrol, secure the perimeter, and break enemy contact. LT hoped to provide more details on our approach because the situation was fluid, as all firefights are. I followed Sergeant Larson aboard the lead bird moments before our pilot pulled up on the yoke. Thus began my first combat air assault onto a hot LZ.

With my M-16 locked and loaded and the radio handset pressed hard to my ear, I listened closely for commo between the pilot and the lurp RTO. I was hoping that by the time we arrived, our howitzers would have broken enemy contact and sent our adversaries running. But as we neared the LZ and the lead pilot requested a sitrep, I could hear crackling rifle fire when the lurp keyed his handset. Obviously, the LZ was still hot.

The lurp said his team had formed a small perimeter around a one-slick, crude LZ and had 01 ambulatory line 2. Redleg was having a positive effect, he said, but that they were still taking fire. He recommended our best direction of approach and signed off. The pilot announced we were going in and gave our ETA to all RTOs. He then called redleg to have them clear tubes. We would go in hard, one bird at a time, and I was in the lead bird. If we made it in safely, another would follow. If we crashed on the LZ, there would be no room for another slick to unload Skytroopers.

Lieutenant Fakler may have been aboard the third slick when he called for 1-3. I answered the call and passed the handset to Sergeant Larson. LT wanted a sitrep as soon as we had boots on the ground.

All slicks descended to treetop level and maintained a high rate of speed. Sergeant Larson tapped me on the shoulder and I moved over so he could sit next to me at the edge of the deck. I looked for the landing zone but saw only treetops race by, just below the skids.

The door gunners opened up with their M-60 machine guns, strafing the jungle canopy. Dozens of empty shell casings spit out the sides of their repeaters. In an instant, the LZ came into view. Lurps were putting down suppressive fire at the edge of a stump-filled hilltop. My heart started pounding faster than the rotor blades were *whoop-whoop*ing. The moment was as exhilarating as it was perilous.

Our pilot dropped in fast. Sergeant Larson stepped down onto a skid. I clipped the radio's handset to my shoulder strap and followed his lead. Skytroopers moved to the open doors to step onto skids or stand at the edge. Everyone was totally exposed. We needed no coaxing to jump from well above the ground, not that the pilot could land anyway with all those tree stumps. Our slick was still moving when everyone began jumping. I landed hard on my feet, barely missing a stump, and immediately started crawling with Sergeant Larson to the edge of the hill. As soon as the last soldier hit the ground, our helicopter banked safely away from the LZ to allow another slick to take its place.

I hunkered down behind a felled tree and took a quick personal inventory, happy to find no exposed bones or unfamiliar holes. I brought the sixteen to my shoulder and began firing indiscriminately downhill. Sergeant Larson took my handset and radioed Lieutenant Fakler, telling him we had boots on the ground. From my vantage point, if we were taking fire it was very light, although it was damn hard to tell from all our shooting and the whooping of rotor blades. Radio communications were almost impossible to hear under such conditions, as was my ability to concentrate on them while I was at the same time trying to kill any motherfucker downhill.

After the last slick pulled away and everyone got into position, we eased up on our shooting to realize return fire had virtually ceased. Charlie had broken contact and was apparently bugging out. Lieutenant Fakler relayed the information to battalion along with a negative casualty report.

Lieutenant Colonel McGraw ordered us downhill to flush out anyone who might hang around to surprise us later. The three squads of 1st Platoon swept downhill on separate courses. In the hour or so it took to clear the area, no squad met resistance. Other than some blood trails, empty shell casings, and fresh tracks going off in different directions, we found little additional evidence of enemy presence. Once again, Charlie had slipped away.

All squads regrouped on the hill where we met the lurp team (minus their medevaced wounded soldier). The small group of about five thanked us for saving their bacon, but I could see they were taking their near-death experience rather casually, even joking about it. All of them looked sharp in their properly fitted camouflage fatigues, face paint, bush hats, and bandannas. One lurp carried a shotgun. Another, the team leader, held out his damaged CAR-15 to show us where an AK round had struck his rifle near the ejection port, causing it to jam. His team members thought it pretty funny how close he came to taking a bullet. Unfazed by their razzing, he pulled out a knife and started digging around the bolt action until it unjammed. Then he pulled back the charging handle, and to our amazement he was able to ram a new round into the chamber. Would it still fire? he wondered aloud. His team advised him not to field-test it, saying the rifle might blow up in his face. Well, that sounded like a challenge to their leader. He flashed a smile and walked to the edge of the hill, where he put the rifle stock next to his thigh and pulled the trigger. *BAM.* The bullet left the barrel. Though the rifle jammed again, he had proven his point. Another smile came to his face and we all grinned back in relief.

It was by now late in the day and Lieutenant Fakler requested our extraction, but his request was denied. I don't recall why, but Lieutenant Colonel McGraw ordered our platoon to stay on the hill overnight. That didn't sit well with anyone because we packed light.

Nobody brought his overnight gear, including ponchos and poncho liners. With only damp fatigues to keep us warm, all we could do was curl up on the ground and hope it wouldn't rain. But of course it did. Without shelter and ponchos, everyone in 1st Platoon suffered in silence until morning when a sortie took us back to LZ Jack. [After the war, Davy Miller told me that in all his twelve months in the field, he never spent a more miserable night than the one on that hill].

Before our next rotation back to the field, Lieutenant Fakler promoted me to platoon RTO. My advancement came as a welcome surprise in that it came so soon. LT liked the way I handled myself during the combat air assault, and he said Sergeant Larson consistently gave me high marks. Their votes of confidence boosted my self-esteem when I needed it most. I savored my first major achievement in company. I also knew more challenges lay ahead.

Platoon RTO

Ipitched my hooch near Lieutenant Fakler's bunker and then milled around the immediate area feeling pretty good about my lot in life—right up until Staff Sergeant Carter caught sight of me. Within earshot of several men, he loudly asked if my name was Phil Harmonica.

"It's Hoffmann, sergeant," I corrected him.

No, he liked Harmonica better and asked if I knew who Phil Harmonica was. No, I admitted, sensing a stinging answer. The platoon sergeant went on to announce that Phil Harmonica was some kind of comic strip character (a claim I have yet to confirm). Snickers rose from the men, which only added salt to the wound. I asked why he would call me that. He leaned toward me and said with a grin, "Because my three up and one down say I can," referring to the number of stripes on the black pins attached to his collar.

Sergeant Carter may have hoped the name would stick, but it never did, I suppose because when you're a radio operator everyone calls you horn, just as all medics are doc. Other than that childish nickname episode, I didn't find Sergeant Carter intolerable. He didn't ride me too hard or otherwise make my life miserable. But what the son of a bitch did that day was diminish me in front of my peers. He reinjured my fragile self-worth by degrading me into some kind of comic strip character. And by doing so, he abused his rank and forgot his history, he being African American.

More pissed than hurt by the platoon sergeant's hazing earlier in the day, I walked alone after sunset to collect my thoughts and ease built-up tension. Along the way I passed a trooper sitting alone atop an earthen bunker smoking a cigarette. "Hi," he said. "Hi," I retuned and kept walking. "Hey, aren't you that radio guy floating around the company?" he called out. I gave him a curt "yeah," thinking his question was just another verbal jab. He called out again and said if I wasn't going anywhere in particular that I ought to join him on the bunker and have a cigarette. Because he sounded sincere, I accepted his offer but declined the smoke.

It so happened we had a long, easy conversation that eventually got around to my antagonist platoon sergeant. He suggested that I not take Sergeant Carter's ribbing personally. Sarge probably kidded all cherries, he said, as if it were a rite of passage. I granted him that Sergeant Carter could consider me new to his platoon, but that I had very little cherry left in me after spending several grueling weeks in company. My skin was deeply tanned, my camouflage helmet cover was faded, my jungle boots were weathered...hell, I even smelled like a veteran of the bush.

I told him why I believed Sergeant Carter's attitude toward me ran deeper than good-natured ribbing: he and others probably saw me as an RTO screw-up who received special treatment from the Old Man. All true at one time, I admitted, but that none of it was true now. Those who still harbored ill will toward me had only to open their closed minds and see that things were different. In the meantime, all I could do was to keep demonstrating my competency on radio and hope to change their tired perceptions.

"Okay, but give Sarge and the others more time; they'll come around," said my new acquaintance. "Things will get better; you'll see."

It felt good opening up to this affable stranger who lent a sympathetic ear. "My name's Phil," I said, when I got up to leave. "What's yours?"

"Everybody calls me Spider," answered the shirtless young man with curly black hair and mustache. Spider was from 4th Platoon, and after that night we only bumped into each other occasionally. Nevertheless, I never forgot his encouraging words.

As always, our stint at LZ Jack ended too soon. While Alpha Company waited patiently at the pickup zone for a sortie to take us back into the field, a giant Skycrane helicopter descended nearby. Strapped beneath it was a heavy 105mm howitzer. As the odd-looking helicopter eased the big cannon to the ground, its long, sweeping overhead blades whipped up a dust storm. We had to turn away as the swirling debris stung our skin and got under our fatigues. Nothing like starting out the day all gritty.

The sortie airlifted us onto a small LZ on the side of a low mountain. After everyone off-loaded, Captain Talbott sent 1st Platoon up the mountainside while all other units worked below us.

Our hump turned into an arduous uphill grind in full gear. By late afternoon the lead squad had reached the mountaintop. From their lofty vantage point, a verdant vista opened before them. Looking down, they saw the Song Be River snake around the base of the mountain. And they saw something else. Moving across the river was some kind of animal, the likes of which the men could only guess. When I got the call, LT and I hurried to see for ourselves. While our drag squad was still working its way up the mountain, LT focused his binoculars on the river crosser and was surprised at what he saw. Slowly moving toward the near shore was a spotted panther.

Some of the men wanted to bag the big cat and asked permission. LT sensed their need to blow off some steam and said okay, but only if the cat had a sporting chance. The participants were restricted to single shots from the hip. Other men, including myself, opted out, although I did watch in grim fascination.

With rifles to their hips, troopers began firing one round after another with each squeeze of their triggers. Bullets pinged the water around the large cat, but it kept swimming. Before the animal reached shore, some of the original critics took up the challenge. Embarrassed to say, I was among them. Soon the panther disappeared downriver with the current, never having made it to shore.

Lieutenant Fakler liked our vantage point on top of the mountain. He also knew the men were beat from the morning's hump. For those reasons, he had the platoon set up a defensive position for the night. Naturally, everyone was in accord with his decision.

Soon after sunset, a brilliant full moon rose in the east casting its glow over the countryside. The temperature began to drop and a light fog rolled in below us obscuring the river. While troopers bedded down, LT and Sergeant Carter stood at the edge of the mountain conversing. As they spoke, a wind came up and the fog began to break. Soon, portions of the river came into view. And then a boat. It was a large, covered sampan floating with the current. No lights were shining from it; only glistening moonlight off the water gave it away.

LT became immediately suspicious of a darkened sampan traveling under the cover of darkness far from any known villages. We were in Indian country, a free fire zone. LT yelled for my radio and I hurried to his side holding out the handset. He called Captain Talbott, who in turn called battalion. Battalion said the vessel was likely transporting NVA along the river using moonlight to guide them. Why else would an unlit sampan try to negotiate the river at night?

Battalion ordered us to engage the boat and to guide in artillery fire. Sergeant Carter yelled for everyone to bring their weapons. Troopers scrambled into position and prepared to lay down fire. Sergeant Roth, a forward observer temporarily assigned to our platoon, busily called in multiple fire missions.

I drew back the charging handle on my sixteen and set it to semi-automatic. With the rifle pressed firmly against my shoulder, I sighted in above the boat, adjusting as I could for distance and downward trajectory. Excitement filled the air as everyone waited for the order to fire. When it came, I began squeezing off the nineteen rounds loaded in my twenty-round magazine, taking quick aim between each shot. [An M-16 rifle was less likely to jam by loading nineteen rounds in a twenty round magazine.] With all the shooting, it was impossible to determine how many of my rounds were hitting the boat or pinging the water around it. Still, I shot expert with an M-16, so I knew many of my rounds were hitting target.

As the sampan neared the bend in the river, artillery got into the act. After several errant rounds and additional adjustments, arty honed in on the wooden vessel. Rudderless and splintered, the sampan disappeared from sight.

The following morning, brigade's commanding general surveyed the area in his C & C before paying us a visit. He took Lieutenant

Fakler aside to glean more information about the incident, but I don't think his junior officer added much to the discussion.

While they conferred, I stayed busy cleaning my rifle and tried not to think about my involvement in both shootings. Each was eating at me, although I could excuse myself for the first. Shooting an exotic animal for kicks in the jungles of Vietnam wasn't criminal; it was just so unnecessary. More troubling to me was the sampan episode. There I willingly fired on unconfirmed targets. Enemy soldiers, if we were to believe battalion. Yet I also knew that the occupants could have been innocent Vietnamese civilians. At the time, the moral implications didn't enter my head. But now, with my conscience bothering me, I questioned my eagerness to pull at the trigger over and over again, taking careful aim at the boat between each shot.

I could find plenty of justifications, like the mob mentality that existed at the time. I also knew that chronically fatigued foot soldiers, especially those operating in hostile environments, could think and behave in ways they normally would not. And then there was the order to shoot—the easiest of all justifications to point at, except I knew better. You see, it wasn't the order to shoot that drew me to fire on the boat; I actually looked forward to the order. If my conscience had bothered me at the time, I could have simply shot up the water. No, the order was only a means to an end. For a host of reasons, I was mad at the world and wanted very much to put some hurt on somebody. Enemy or no enemy, those aboard the sampan became convenient targets of my pent-up anger.

After the general left our mountaintop, 1st Platoon saddled up and continued along the ridgeline. Our intention was to rendezvous with the company in a day or two. Late that afternoon, LT found a suitable area to set up for the night. While squads formed a small defensive perimeter, our CP took up center position. I cleared a piece of ground, including a scorpion hiding under a rock, and put down a ground cloth.

At one point, a trooper walked over from his squad to see Doc. He had a large boil on the back of his neck that was giving him a headache. After examining the bulbous, walnut-sized node, Doc recommended the trooper fly to Camp Evans to have a doctor lance it. The GI balked at letting anyone put a knife to the tender growth. Besides that, he wasn't about to leave his squad. Doc predicted the boil would continue to grow and eventually need medical attention anyway, but his words fell on deaf ears. The suffering trooper accepted aspirin before walking back to his unit.

In the middle of the night, while sitting up against a tree during radio watch, I thought about home and the letters tucked away inside my helmet liner. Their tangible presence brought back a sense of balance to my life in an unbalanced world. I could not imagine serving one day longer than necessary in Vietnam, and yet there were men here who had volunteered to extend their tours.

At first light, 1st Platoon prepared for another long day of humping heavy. I called 6 India to request a log bird and then went on to finish cinching my gear. After the resupply helicopter delivered water to fill our canteens, Lieutenant Fakler gave the order to saddle up and we continued down the ridgeline.

At some point along the hump, I got a call from lead squad to say they spotted a flashing light on the opposite bank. LT and I walked up to have a look. Within the distant trees there was indeed a flashing light. Some of the men thought a gook was signaling in Morse code to warn his buddies on our side of the river. I watched for a few seconds to be sure and then announced to everyone that if the signal was in code, it wasn't Morse. Score one for me.

LT yelled for a "thumper," and a couple of troopers came forward carrying M-79 grenade launchers. He challenged them to lob fragmentation grenades onto the distant target and both eagerly took up the challenge. Together, they raised their stubby, wide-barreled rifles skyward knowing they would need every bit of their weapons' 400-meter range. In near unison, they pulled their triggers. *Poomp-poomp*. Within seconds, collective groans rose from the peanut gallery after both grenades burst short of target.

We fully expected the noise to scare anyone away, and yet the flashing continued. LT next ordered in small-arms fire to aid the thumpers. Riflemen had the distance to target, if not the desired result. When the cease-fire order came and the flashing continued, we knew for sure a mirror or shiny metal was hanging in a tree flashing in the breeze. The question now became, why was it there? Lieutenant Fakler reported the situation to Captain Talbott, who thought the object was an enemy waypoint marker. The CO put in a request to have a Cobra gunship fly out and obliterate it. When the attack helicopter arrived on scene, it swooped in on target and fired its rockets. Needless to say, the light shone no more.

Early that evening, 1st Platoon set up a night defensive position on the side of a forested knoll. Troopers busied themselves with their customary assignments, including stocky Sergeant Roth who was calculating DTs. When I finished performing commo checks and penny counts with the squads, Captain Talbott and Lieutenant Fakler got on the horn to discuss our next day's hump. After dark, 1st Platoon settled in for some needed sleep.

During my late night radio watch, a trooper whispered to me over his handset that he could hear movement outside the wire. Calls of this nature were not all that uncommon in the bush; they usually came in reaction to nocturnal animals moving through the jungle. Wait long enough and the animal either walked away or tripped a flare, with the latter always getting everyone's attention. I whispered back and asked if he had a visual. "Negative," he responded. I suggested he alert his squad leader if the noise continued. I then advised the other squads to stay sharp.

A couple minutes passed before the squad leader called to say they were hearing multiple movements outside the wire. He wanted to send up an illumination flare but dense tree canopy made that impossible. I said, "Wait one" and scrambled in the dark to alert Lieutenant Fakler. LT recovered quickly from his sleep and had me fetch Sergeant Carter. They consulted before LT ordered the sectors closest to the movement to prepare for a "mad minute" (concentration of fire from all weapons at maximum rate for sixty seconds). As troopers readied themselves, Sergeant Carter made his way down to supervise.

I was standing between LT and Sergeant Roth when LT brought the handset up to his mouth. Just as he was about to issue the order to fire, a trip flare went off outside the perimeter launching the mad minute without voice command.

A fusillade of weaponry instantly turned the jungle into an outrageous display of noise and light. Exploding claymores echoed under jungle canopy. Muzzles flashed. Red tracer rounds danced off trees. M-79 grenades exploded prematurely off treetops, making them a poor choice of weapon in such close quarters.

The three of us stood shoulder to shoulder watching the dazzling light show when we noticed something missing in it. There were no green tracer rounds returning our direction from enemy AK rifles. LT decided to call off the mad minute and ordered an immediate ceasefire. As the shooting came to an end, a final M-79 grenade burst high off a branch. At almost the same instant, both Lieutenant Fakler and Sergeant Roth cried out in pain before they crumpled to my feet. Sergeant Roth rolled on the ground writhing in pain as our platoon leader lay quiet and motionless. I dropped to my knees and swept the ground in the dark for the handset. "CEASE FIRE, DAMMIT! CEASE FIRE!" I finally yelled into the mouthpiece.

Doc was nearby to give aid. He pointed his flashlight on Sergeant Roth and saw him gripping his leg. Seeing little blood, he turned to our unconscious platoon leader. Blood was running down LT's hairline onto his face. It looked bad. Doc grabbed a field bandage from his medical pouch and began wiping away the blood, trying to find an entry wound. While he worked, I radioed Sergeant Carter to come back to our location ASAP.

Fortunately for LT, his wound was minor. Shrapnel from the M-79 grenade had struck only a glancing blow to his head. It was hard enough, though, to knock him out and produce a substantial amount of blood. Doc bandaged the lieutenant's head and then turned his attention to Sergeant Roth. A small piece of shrapnel had entered the FO's upper left thigh lodging deep into muscle, but it had missed the femoral artery and bone. Doc cleaned the wound and secured it with a field bandage. He thought both men could wait until morning for a medevac.

Only after the perimeter settled down did I realize how lucky my "bookends" were. Had Lieutenant Fakler cocked his head two inches closer to mine at the time of the tree burst, he would have likely died. And had Sergeant Roth stood only inches farther from me, we would still be searching the ground for his testicles. And had I been standing just a tad one direction or the other....

At first light, troopers checked the perimeter to see what caused the overnight hubbub and passed along their findings to me. I relayed the info to our company RTO, saying we found several pounds of ground venison. Lieutenant Fakler complained only of a minor headache. Doc thought he suffered a slight concussion and recommended a medevac take him out, but LT refused. Sergeant Roth did require additional medical attention, but we didn't have a suitable LZ to land a helicopter. When someone suggested a medevac extract him using a harness and cable, Sergeant Roth said no. He was ambulatory and convinced Doc he could walk with the aid of a sturdy stick until we came across a suitable LZ.

The hump began well enough for Sergeant Roth. He was able to walk behind me and keep pace with the aid of a walking stick. But as the morning wore on, his injured thigh muscle began to tighten, and he frequently lost ground. More than once I had to radio our point man and ask him to slow down or stop until the FO hobbled back into position. By the end of the morning's hump, Sergeant Roth's bad leg had stiffened at the knee to where he had to hop on his good leg while putting full pressure on the stick. The guy was in obvious distress, but he never complained.

During midday chow, the FO admitted he could no longer walk. LT apprised Captain Talbott, who ordered us to clear an LZ. He would extract not only the FO but also the entire platoon. To that end, a log bird arrived on scene and lowered chain saws through the trees. Troopers immediately put the chain saws to use while others cleared brush. The rest of the platoon stood down, away from falling trees.

While the clearing progressed, the GI with the boil on his neck sought Doc for treatment. Doc re-examined the inflamed nodule, noting it had ballooned to the size and color of a plum. It definitely needed medical attention and so Doc insisted that the GI accompany Sergeant Roth back to Camp Evans. Again the obstinate grunt refused to separate from his squad, but this time he would allow our platoon medic to lance it. Doc argued against the idea amid cheers of encouragement from the swelling crowd who had come to gawk. There was just no denying their lust for pus. In fact, some men pulled out their knives and said if Doc didn't have the stomach for it, they would gladly do the cutting. Probably to save the suffering GI's neck from the lynch mob, Doc reluctantly agreed to perform surgery and opened his medical pouch.

Someone who had seen too many western movies offered the GI a bullet to bite on, but Doc didn't want his work complicated by cracked teeth. Someone else shaved a stick to serve the purpose.

Doc held the tip of a sharp knife over the flame of a Zippo lighter. He then doused the blade and the man's neck in alcohol to finish the sterilization process. In final preparation for surgery, a couple of troopers immobilized the GI in a headlock and bear hug. Spectators crowded closer as Doc brought the knife up to the bulbous mass. An anticipatory hush fell over the crowd.

When the tip of the knife touched the boil, it was like a pin pricking an overfilled water balloon. Stinking pus spewed out onto Doc's face and chest. He reeled in disgust choking back vomit, sounding like a dog trying to yak up septic road kill—ugga-ugga-ugga. The patient howled in pain. Spectators whirled in revulsion.

Doc interrupted surgery only long enough to regain control over his gag reflex and to clean himself up. Then, remaining true to his profession, he went on to finish the procedure. Over the patient's protest, Doc pinched the purulent wound until he found what he was looking for. Again he took up the knife. He stuck the tip of it into the open sore and dug out the large, bloody core. With a triumphant look, he held up the mass as if it were a trophy for all to see before flicking it unceremoniously into the bushes where it hung like a Christmas ornament. After a little more pinching, he cleaned and bandaged the wound. The operation now over, the shaken but grateful GI returned to his squad without postoperative complications.

Doc didn't know it, but another GI would soon need his services. Amid the sounds of whining chain saws and trees crashing in the jungle, a man clearing brush didn't notice a tree falling his direction. I was down path listening to another tree crack under its own weight when over the noise came the most horrific series of shrieks imaginable. I grabbed my ruck, and along with everyone else, raced toward the commotion.

At the partially cut LZ, troopers were huddling over Spin, the injured man. He was conscious and moaning after a large tree limb struck him on the back, paralyzing him from the waist down. I put in a priority request with our company RTO for a medevac to pick up a line 2 with a spinal injury and possible internal injuries. Company CP passed the call to battalion and they in turn requested the medevac.

In the little time it took for the evacuation helicopter to arrive, our tree cutters had yet to clear an opening. Because time was critical, Lieutenant Fakler felt he had no choice but to stop the cutting and have the pilot lower a rigid jungle penetrator. The metal basket would immobilize Spin in a prone position while a cable lifted him into the chopper. But there was a problem. The medevac had brought only a canvas litter, a poor substitute for someone with broken vertebra. Doc said there wasn't time to go back for a basket and convinced LT to proceed with the extraction.

The helicopter crew lowered the canvas litter through the trees at the end of a cable. When the litter reached the ground, troopers unsnapped the cable and tightly wrapped the canvas around Spin's torso. Then they reconnected the cable and gave thumbs up to the hovering helicopter. As the cable tightened, Spin tilted vertically while troopers tried to keep him rigid inside the canvas cocoon. Slowly, Spin rose through their fingertips until he was free of ground assist. The litter began to sway, brushing up against tree branches until it reached the floor of the medevac. Two crewmen reached down and began pulling Spin inside, and in so doing, they bent him at the waist. Wild screams echoed over the beating chopper blades. I had to turn away, unable to watch the sickening sight.

After the medevac left, troopers once again took up their chain saws. By late afternoon, we had a suitable LZ for choppers to execute a pickup. First Platoon was reunited with Alpha Company, and Sergeant Roth flew back to Camp Evans for treatment.

Our company remained in the field a full rotation before returning to LZ Jack. On our first day back at camp, Lieutenant Fakler took me aside to say I performed well in the field, and that he had told Captain Talbott as much. I expressed my thanks for his vote of confidence. He smiled and added, "The CO wants to see you."

"You mean he wants me back as his radioman?" I asked.

"Possibly. That's what he wants to talk to you about."

What sweet music to my ears. I thanked the lieutenant again (this time more profoundly) and grabbed my gear. As I started to double-time it, he shouted for me to unstrap the radio from my ruck. "We'll need that one, Hoffmann. The CO may have another for you."

Filled with anticipation, I hurried to the company bunker where Captain Talbott was waiting. He sat me down and asked if I was ready to reassume the position of company RTO, to which I responded with an instant and enthusiastic yes.

"Not so fast," he cautioned, saying my answer required serious thought. What if my return proved premature, he asked? Could I accept the stigma of a second demotion if I failed again?

I easily dismissed his question, because for me there was really nothing to consider. Failure—a word never associated with me at Fort Huachuca—had pretty much defined me in Alpha Company, at least until a few short weeks ago. Here I had been scrutinized, stigmatized, traumatized, everything but homogenized. Granted, most of my failures were self-inflicted. But the thing is, as bad as things got, I never gave up. My precipitous fall from grace had ultimately toughened me, not further weakened me. And now that I had proven myself at squad and platoon levels, I felt sure I could surmount one final challenge. If ever I hoped to get out of the bush and operate Lieutenant Colonel McGraw's radio at battalion, I would first have to succeed as company RTO. So fear to fail be damned; there was no way in hell I was about to pass up this, and possibly my last opportunity to serve at the captain's side.

"I'm ready this time, sir," I said in a firm voice. With a nod of his head, Captain Talbott accepted me back to the company CP.

Company RTO Redux

It seems Captain Talbott based my promotion on something more than performance. Potter had served his tour of duty and only recently left the company to return home. His job slot went to Gilmore, which opened the company radio position to me. I had to wonder what would have happened had Potter's tour ended months later. Would I have been stuck in 1st Platoon? Yes or no, it didn't matter now. Bottom line, I earned my way back to company level, and this time no one lost his job because of me.

It is now late October 1968 and MACV is in the midst of instituting the largest tactical redeployment of the Vietnam War. Increased activity by well-armed North Vietnamese Army divisions along the Ho Chi Minh Trail gives rise to Allied suspicions that the communists are preparing for another Tet offensive. In response to the potential threat, MACV orders the entire 1st Cavalry Division (Airmobile) to quick deploy from northern I Corps to III Corps near the Cambodian border. By mid-November, our division would be in place to interdict enemy infiltration routes running toward Saigon, South Vietnam's capital city.

Alpha Company's next trip to the field would be its last in I Corps before redeployment south. Choppers flew us into the piedmont, where the terrain was more open and flat. The Old Man saw this as an opportunity to cover more ground, and so he split off two platoons.

At days end, the CP and its remaining platoons—one rifle and one mortar—formed a night defensive position on the side of a gently sloping hill dotted by trees. The two other rifle platoons also took positions on the hill: one set up far above us and the other set up far below us, although both were in our view. At dusk, all men were reported inside their perimeters.

The company FO calculated defensive targets beginning with the platoon below us and relayed the data to arty. A cannon on LZ Jack fired a white phosphorous ground-burst to verify the calculation. Soon, white, burning tentacles explode off the ground closer to the platoon than the FO had hoped, but still at a safe distance. Or so we thought. While the FO recalculated, the downhill platoon RTO called to have us hold off any more DTs until they accounted for all their pennies. His announcement caught us by surprise, for only minutes earlier he had cleared our request. A frowning Captain Talbott picked up the handset and wanted an explanation from his platoon leader. When the lieutenant came on the horn, he said a GI had sneaked outside the perimeter to defecate. After finishing his business, the truant trooper started back to the perimeter when the willy peter exploded...on top of his feces! The startled GI said he was lucky the explosion didn't catch him with his pants down. LT promised to reprimand the GI. With a chuckle, he said, "Not to worry, six, I'll jump his shit."

One day our direction took us along a river to a wide, sandy beach. The company had been there before, and when we reached it, anticipation filled the air. I called a company niner-niner and relayed the order to break for chow. As soon as my message went out, troopers let out a holler and began shedding equipment and clothes. RTOs and a few others stood sentry in sweaty contempt as the rest of the company ran down the beach in varying stages of undress to cool in the river. Our turn would come, though. When it did, I stripped down and ran barefoot over the hot sand, plunging into the water for a rare bath.

On still another day out, we came to a narrow part of the river represented by a blue line on the map. The Old Man said we needed to get to the other side. He had a few men remove their rucks and look for a shallow crossing, but not halfway across the approximately twenty-five-meter span, all found themselves struggling against the current wet to their armpits. The CO next sent squads in opposite directions along the bank to locate a suitable fording point. When they returned shaking their heads, Captain Talbott had run out of good options.

His next plan of action smacked of desperation when he ordered the entire company to cross the river suspended under ropes. First, he had a volunteer drop his gear, wrap a rope around his waist, and swim to the opposite shore. There he shinnied up a tree and tied off his end of the rope. We did the same thing on our side of the river, making sure the rope was taut.

It was now time to test Talbott's folly. A GI attached his ruck to the suspended rope using a carabiner. From behind the ruck, he grabbed the rope with both hands and slung his legs over it.

Hanging upside down, he began moving in inchworm fashion, pushing his ruck forward with his feet. All went swimmingly at first, but the farther he inched over the water, the lower the rope sagged. Soon, his buns were cooling in the river. By the time he was halfway across, only his head and feet were visible. At that point, all but the captain and rope crosser laughed like hell.

While we were busy pretending to be Navy SEALS, a couple of smiling troopers came into view on the opposite shore. They were wet to the waist and waving their arms. Without permission, they had worked their way along the bank testing the water's depth at different intervals until they found a suitable crossing. I thought the enterprising troopers deserved medals for saving us from having to make dugout canoes or Huck Finn rafts.

Lighter moments such as these helped to break up tension and boredom, but humping the bush was always a serious business. And while I can't recall Alpha Company engaging in any protracted firefights during that short rotation, we likely encountered small enemy run-ins and booby traps. By the end of October, Alpha Company was back at LZ Jack performing day recons.

The following comes from a battalion operational report. I'm guessing the referred-to meeting was in reference to orders from 3rd Brigade, call sign Garry Owen, concerning the massive redeployment of the 1st Cavalry Division (Airmobile).

> 1 Nov 68
> cp & 1-6 moves e s/e 1k.
> 0720H
> 2-6 4-6 jack.
> 1223H
> message from garry owen 6 have co ready for on call meeting.

As I mentioned earlier, daily operational reports stored in our national archives after the war were missing large blocks of dates relating to my time in country. The following descriptions come from available reports and involve Delta Company on 1 and 2 November 1968. Alpha Company is also mentioned. I use these reports to show the kind of activity all 5th Battalion companies experienced while operating around LZ Jack. Bracketed material is for clarification.

1 nov 69
1332H
2-6 finds booby trap. 1 us [U.S.] frag in c-rats can and wire across trail recent activity in area.
operation jeb stuart III ao [area of operation] in piedmont in vicinity of evans & east on the coastal plain. a [Alpha] co lz jack recon and ambush patrols.

2 nov 69
0913H
1-6 509255 [map grid] finds 08 odd od [olive drab] rags 02 pj pants inside 105 canister. 01 white blouse khaki shirt 01 black handbag 01 us sand bag 01 lrg piece plastic 02 btl salt. neg sign recent activity.
1-6 tripped booby trap consisting of us frag in fruit can w/ trip wire across trail. req medevac 2 em [enlisted men] wia 01 litter 01 ambulatory line 40 [soldier ID] line 90 wia.
1210H
1-6 bunker line 09 made of logs 01 5x8 sand bags & tin roof 02 4x4x4 made of logs and dirt 03 hooches near bunkers 01 observation platform in tree 03 us helmet liners 01 fired law [Light Anti-Armor Weapon] 01 us poncho 04 water dippers 03 fish traps 02 metal pots 01 us flak jacket 01 pair sandals. neg sign of recent activity.
1450H
1-6 400-450 lbs unpolished rice in 50 burlap sacks unspoiled 50-60 lbs polished rice 01 us conus 01 pair black pants 02 nva shirts green 01 water proof camo cover 10 lbs salt 01 piece of blue cloth 01 parachute 61 type 3 female blouses 02 green 01 white 01 protective mask cover gi 01 us canteen 01 burlap sack w/ heat tabs. area camouflaged. activity approx 1 week ago.
2100H
D co 3-2 ambush has trip flare go off observed movement engaged w/s/a [with small arms] m-79 enemy evaded south 4-5 indiv results: 01 enemy kia no weapons no us casualties indiv kia wearing gi fatigue shirt black shorts gi canteen w/ cover gook poncho 50 piasters 02 ball point pens 01 cig lighter armed w/ 02 gi frags tobacco & paper & pouch 01 pair glasses 01 nva

pistol belt indiv carrying 02 chickens indiv full of small arms and frag holes.

There was no mention in the report on the status of the chickens. I'm guessing Delta's 2nd Squad held the poultry for interrogation...then ate them.

> Operations summary: 5/7 continued to conduct combat operations in jeb stuart III area of op. op in piedmont & vicinity of camp evans & east to the coastal plain.
> A co continues security of fb [firebase] jack conducted night ambushes & recon s/se & n/ne.
> Statistical summary: friendly casualties kia 0 wia 2.
> Cumulative op total: kia 19 wia 108 enemy casualties kia 171 est add 82 pow 2 ch 2 cd 2 friendly equip loses 0 enemy equip 0 # of ambushes 14 as of 2 nov 68.
> Closing location: A co at jack 1-6, 3-6, 3-1, out.

On 5 November, Alpha Company conducted mine sweeps on the road from LZ Jack to Camp Evans. Also on that day, our nation elected Richard Nixon president. He promised an honorable and speedy end to the war. Neither happened.

On 6 November, Alpha Company mobilized at Camp Evans in preparation for our move south into III Corps. The division had already begun its redeployment into an area northwest of Saigon near the Cambodian border. Our mission there was to interdict the enemy pushing through III Corps from war-neutral Cambodia toward Saigon. Captain Talbott said we should expect some heavy fighting in our next area of operation (AO).

Months before my arrival in Vietnam, the 1st Cav and other U. S. military had already rooted out major staging areas in I and II Corps once held with impunity by the communists. As a partial result of these military successes, the enemy relied more heavily on the Ho Chi Minh Trail system to move men and materiel toward Saigon. These trail systems ran within the adjacent countries of Laos and Cambodia.

President Nixon eventually authorized limited aerial bombing along the trails in an effort to stop the free flow of men and materiel, however the tactic had mixed results. Our resourceful enemy adapted by moving under the cover of darkness and under dense jungle canopy that hid much of the trail from the air. For our country to effectively prosecute the war, we needed U.S. ground forces inside those adjacent borders to engage enemy strongholds. At that time, however, Nixon would not allow combat troops into those sovereign countries. The administration remained concerned over world condemnation if we expanded the war. And then there was China to consider. It threatened to enter the war if we sent troops into North Vietnam. Our government's policy decisions effectively hamstrung the U.S. military and allowed the communist North to exploit our policy of limited war. North Vietnamese regulars thus established elaborate staging areas inside Cambodia along III Corps, the shortest distance from Cambodia to Saigon. The First Team would soon tangle with the likes of the well-outfitted 1st and 7th NVA Divisions and the battle-seasoned 5th and 9th VC Divisions.

Not until May of 1970 did Washington officially send U.S. ground forces into Cambodia, and then only temporarily. The mighty 1st Cav got the assignment and inflicted some serious payback on the enemy, smashing their once safe havens. But at that time, Washington was seeking what it called an "honorable" conclusion to an unpopular American war. Its priorities had changed—changed from winning the conflict to containing it in hopes of reaching a peace accord with the North. If Washington could accomplish its goal, the war would end, the people at home could put the war (and those who fought in it) behind them, and history books might spare our leaders' names from the stigma of utter defeat rather than a negotiated settlement. How nice and sanitized, unless one considers what happened in the meantime. Until all U.S. military forces left Vietnam three years later through the peace talks, Washington continued to send thousands of young Americans to fight in a war it did not intend to win. During those same years, our government replaced the draft with a draft lottery, which forced approximately 850,000 additional men to put their lives on the line. Not for the sake of freedom, for the sake of saving face.

When I served in Vietnam, Washington's official line was to win the war, even though many, if not most of us who were doing the fighting, believed our current policy was doomed to fail. I mentioned this in a letter I sent to Ron around the time of our move south. The tone of it clearly shows a young soldier worried about upcoming events:

> Man you're lucky as hell you're not over here. I work my balls off seven days a week in the damn field. To make it worse, I'm a grunt with a radio. We're out of the mountains now and working the flat lands. Being in the flats is no picnic. A few men have been killed and a lot wounded by booby traps. It sure sobers a guy up seeing good men die in front of you for seemingly no cause at all. No one is winning this damn war. Writing letters home depresses the hell out of me. I think about home and messing around with you again and I'd do about anything to get back there. I'm tired of being shot at.
>
> The First Cav. Div. is moving south in a couple of days. Only the "higher ups" know why. The Cav. only moves when there's trouble brewing. This is one of the biggest operations for any one in Nam. Bigger than A Shaw Valley or Hue where the Cav. wiped the gooks out. We think we're going in preparation for another Tet offensive. We think this one will be before Christmas. Up here we just had to worry about gooks in small numbers. Down there is where the action is. That's where we find battalions of gooks in battle. There are going to be a lot of people killed down there. I just looked over this and it sounds as if I'm trying to make you feel sorry for me. I'm not! Once I got here I knew I would be coming back. Being with the captain as his radio op I'm near the action, but most of the time not in it. I'm just telling you like it is.
>
> Christmas is coming up. I'm expecting a bottle from you of course. If you don't drink it first. Make it a small one if you decide to send one. And wrap it well. A fellow got two fifths one day – BROKEN. We both cried all day. What's a letter without a poem.
>
> > Jingle Bells, mortar shells
> > VC in the grass
> > You can take your Merry Christmas
> > And shove it up your ass

The companies of 5ᵗʰ Battalion waited on the tarmac for C-130 aircraft to ferry us south in Operation Liberty Canyon. After waiting for what seemed like hours under a blazing sun, two companies—including Alpha—moved to the edge of the runway as instructed. While the other company climbed aboard the ass end of their C-130, we waited for the next plane out. Once loaded, the first plane turned sharply onto the runway, putting our company directly behind its engines. The pilot went full throttle and the blast of air from those big props literally tumbled men head over heels. Equipment flew everywhere. Those cockpit cocksuckers probably laughed well down the runway before we dared get up to shake ourselves off.

Troopers searched the area for their own stuff. My heart sank when I found my helmet. All my letters and pictures were gone. Many of the guys experienced similar losses. Our tangible connections to home looked like nothing more than roadside debris. In the short time it took our plane to move into position, we grabbed anything within reach to sort out later. Everyone hurried up the ramp and sat on the metal floor for the uncomfortable 965-kilometer ride south.

III Corps

Fifth Battalion gathered at newly established 3rd Brigade headquarters at Quan Loi, located several kilometers east of the Cambodian border in the Binh Long Province. Also known as Camp Andy, Quan Loi would serve as 5th Battalion's rear headquarters. The battalion's forward headquarters and TOC would later deploy to an outlying firebase.

Division's base of operations was headquartered farther southeast at Phuoc Vinh (Camp Gorvad). From there, division established mutually supportive firebases inside Tay Ninh Province under operation Sheridan Sabre. Our mission was to interdict infiltration routes in the Tong Thang II AO along the Cambodian border in an area known as the Fishhook.

A French rubber plantation abutted Quan Loi. Within it, symmetrically planted rubber trees exposed wide, mostly uncluttered corridors. Dense tree canopy kept much of the plantation floor eerily dusk-like, even under the brightest sun. Those who spent any time at camp would surely remember all that red dirt; it clung to everything. Many of the buildings had wood sides and floors covered by metal roofs. I looked forward to sleeping off the ground and would have gladly finished my tour right there, notwithstanding a welcome wagon greeting from the Viet Cong. They dropped in between twenty and thirty 82mm mortar rounds soon after our arrival, as reported in battalion logs.

On our first mission from camp, a sortie airlifted Alpha Company southwest of Quan Loi. As usual, arty prepped the area before we entered a large clearing covered in elephant grass.

My company had participated in so many helicopter insertions that troopers had come to treat them almost casually, at least from my perspective. During the short time I served in northern I Corps, seldom did we take fire on landings, and when we did, it was sporadic. But after our move south to III Corps, rifle companies took ground insertions very seriously, especially after what happened to 2nd Battalion's Delta Company. On 3 December, a sortie inserted Delta onto an open field fifteen kilometers northeast of Quan Loi. Arty had just prepped the LZ prior to the company's insertion to limit the chance of enemy ambush. Normally an effective tactic, it proved otherwise on that day. What Delta Company didn't know was that four hundred heavily armed NVA were hiding in ambush within wood line bunkers.

At an almost three-to-one man advantage over Delta, the enemy patiently waited until all Skytroopers exited their slicks. It was then they opened up with a barrage of small-arms fire, B-40 rockets, and 82mm mortars. The men of Delta Company were caught in the open with only tall elephant grass for cover. If not for the Cavalry's quick-strike capabilities, the company was at risk of annihilation. Troopers on the ground called in artillery and helicopter gunships. Navy F-4 Phantom jets scrambled to the scene. After nearly five hours of fighting, our combined efforts forced the enemy to withdraw, but not before Delta Company sustained near fifty percent casualties. The after-action report noted there were twenty-three American soldiers killed and another fifty-two wounded.

Fortunately for Alpha Company, four hundred heavily armed Asians with bad intentions weren't peering at us through gun sights as our slicks approached. We would, however, still feel their presence that morning—and almost at my expense.

Skytroopers jumped into the elephant grass and purposely moved toward the wood line. The CP took up a medial position inside the clearing, next to clumps of bushes and a few scrub trees. When I saw Captain Talbott pull out his map and a cigarette, I took advantage of the down time and sat up against a scrub tree to relieve weight from my shoulders. A trooper stood next to me and we spoke casually. Suddenly his calm expression turned severe. He stepped back and stretched out an arm, turning the palm of his hand up like a traffic cop.

"Don't move, Horn," he warned.

"Why, what's wrong?" I demanded.

"Just...don't...move."

My heart quickened. "Don't be fuckin' with me, man. What's it, a snake?"

His next two words caught my breath.

"Booby trap!"

Booby trap?! Holy shit! No wonder the look on his face and why I'm about to piss my pants. All of a sudden that scrub tree wasn't so comfortable. In fact, I had this overwhelming urge to get up and run, but dared not.

Why it is I don't know, but when someone says don't move, my instinct is to do otherwise. A great example comes from many years later when I was about to get a vasectomy. As the doctor was poised to thrust a hypodermic needle the size of a javelin deep into my scrotum to numb my nuts, he says, "Don't move."

Really Doc? You really think it's necessary to say don't move when I can see you're about to bury that needle deep into my sac? What exactly do you think I'm going to do, jiggle my boys? I realize that after you snip and cauterize the vasa deferentia, my balls will be little more than flotsam between my legs, but hell, I still like 'em. So while I may have this overwhelming urge to bolt off this table and run pants-less down the corridor, you needn't worry, Doc, 'cause I ain't movin'.

This current situation was only slightly different in that I had more to lose than my still-functioning family jewels. Speaking of which, Captain Talbott proved he had big ones for staying with me after he ordered everyone else away.

I was having an out-of-body experience while the Old Man quietly assessed the situation. The tension was palpable. Finally I had to ask, "Is it a grenade?"

"It's a large warhead of some kind," he said, showing a look of concern. "It's rigged to the back of the scrub you're leaning against... so don't move."

Warhead? I found the word difficult to process. It sounded a whole lot more ominous than a grenade, although realistically, the means of death by either explosive was irrelevant in light of my distance from it. Dead is dead, after all. About the only difference between the two blasts would be the manner in which Dorothy and Burt would receive their son's remains—in a body bag or a pickle jar.

According to Captain Talbott, had the enemy rigged the device to explode remotely, we'd be dead already. Oh great, I feel so much better now, like a condemned man might feel sitting in the electric chair hearing he has a stay while the executioner is stuck in traffic.

The Old Man saw no wires coming off the device and concluded it was most likely a concussion bomb, set to explode when a careless grunt—in this example, me—bumped the scrub it was attached to. He thought my best approach was not to attempt to slip out of the harness, but to lean forward away from the scrub still wearing the ruck. When I agreed, there was nothing more to say. The Old Man wished me well and walked away at a brisk pace, leaving me alone to extricate myself.

I was scared, really scared, to the point of trembling, which under the circumstances was not a good thing. With no time to waste, I slowly...ever so slowly...leaned forward. My mind spun like a roulette wheel. *Round and round she goes, when she blows, nobody knows.*

At some point, my ruck cleared the tree and I rolled onto my hands and knees, pausing a moment to take in a couple of deep breaths. Then, with some difficulty, I stood on weak legs and started to walk unsteadily toward the men. On the way, I glanced over my shoulder and saw the bomb mostly hidden from view. I cursed myself for not seeing it earlier. Hard to say, but the warhead may have been about two feet long, several inches wide, flat at the bottom, and conical at the top.

A few of the guys came out of the tree line to escort me back, and of course they had to throw in some verbal jabs. Some were even good-natured. Because the warhead didn't explode, most men thought it was old and probably a dud. Naturally we couldn't depend on that theory, so two troopers remained behind to detonate the device.

When the company had moved out of view of the LZ, we heard a small explosion, followed immediately by a larger blast. The warhead was not a dud after all. And so it seemed my sorry ass was but a bump away from becoming elephant grass fertilizer. When the two troopers caught up to us, they looked at me with crooked smiles as if to say I really dodged a bullet, or so to speak.

Compared to I Corps, maneuvers in III Corps were easier on us physically in that the terrain was flatter and more open. Other than that, little else had appeal. We humped more ground and discovered more bunker complexes. Some contained large caches of weapons, food, and medical supplies. There were also more stagnant, leech-infested waters in the south than the clear mountain streams we came across in the north.

While I had yet to experience a protracted firefight against a force equal to or larger than that of our own company, I felt it was only a matter of time. Until then, we would experience an increase in guerilla tactics, booby traps, and the bane of higher casualties.

On one of our days out, the company entered a village along a prescribed route, and like all "villes," we approached it cautiously. We were looking for young, military-aged men our Kit Carson could question, but as with most villages, the population mostly consisted of old men, women, and children. Men of military age usually disappeared or hid before our arrival. Or they were already away soldiering for one side or the other.

There are stories about American soldiers harassing villagers (or worse), including setting fires to their thatched huts, but I never witnessed any of that during my stint in Alpha Company. We acted professionally, even though villagers were known to aid and abet the communists.

When entering this particular ville, we spotted a young Vietnamese man running away through an open field. He was not carrying a weapon, and he didn't stop when our Kit Carson gave the order. Troopers drew a bead on the suspected VC. Villagers screamed in alarm.

"Hold your fire!" yelled the captain over my handset. "He's unarmed!" Men wanted to dispatch the runaway, but the captain had it right. Without a weapon, the villager might have been only a frightened civilian. I thought it was a wise decision coming from our leader. He didn't bend to the constant drumbeat from battalion to raise body counts.

Days later, Alpha Company entered a marsh rich in vegetation and trees. Platoons flanked both sides of the main body as all three columns slogged through calf-high, stagnant water. I got a call from Davy Miller, lead platoon RTO in my column, who said they stopped because an alligator or crocodile was lying in the water only a few meters to their front. The CO wanted to see for himself, and of course Gilmore and I shadowed him up the line. Sure enough, when we got to the front and looked out ahead we saw a crocodile-like creature facing us with only its eyes, nose, and part of its ridged back exposed in the water. Someone said it might be a caiman, a smaller crocodilian cousin. Call it whatever, it looked dangerous, and here we were standing in its habitat.

Davy kicked at the water in his attempt to scare the critter away. It didn't budge. He stepped closer. Curiosity got the better of me, and the two of us advanced, splashing and kicking with each step. Still, the ominous creature didn't move. "Maybe it's dead," I suggested. We slogged ahead a few more steps, kicking and splashing. Again, the reptile of ancient ancestry remained motionless. From behind, someone called us back. Davy exercised good judgment and turned while I stubbornly made one final attempt to coax the critter out of our way. From the water I picked up a floating stick and flung it, hitting the reptile on its back. Well, that was all the giddy-up it needed. Water erupted around the reptile as its powerful tail propelled it directly—*Oh shit!*—toward me.

Without turning around, I backpedaled through the marsh to escape the beast but found myself grossly overmatched. In self-defense, I raised my M-16, flipped the safety to full automatic, and took quick aim. Just as I was about to rock 'n' roll on the critter (now only a few short meters from striking), it suddenly scooted off to the left, leaving me in its wake. I spun around and immediately slammed into Captain Talbott, almost knocking him into the water. Laughter echoed throughout the marsh, and even the Old Man and I had to laugh. Like it or not, between my antics with the reptile and the earlier warhead incident, I had unintentionally become the company's headline entertainer.

Contending with leeches was a common thing for foot soldiers in Nam, but I can tell you we never got used to it. Okay, at least I never got used to it. Still, I've seen brave men shiver when removing them. I recall this particular day when we had to cross a small, turbid stream, the height of which came to our chests. After struggling up the muddy embankment on the opposite side, everyone checked under their muddy fatigues for those large Asian bloodsuckers, as was our routine after such water crossings. A chorus of groans went out. We had hit the mother lode of leeches, reaching from nipples to ankles.

Wet rucks and fatigues began dropping to the ground. Top Shaffer, that tough-as-nails veteran of three wars, stood there naked as a jaybird, covered in goose bumps and leeches, each the size of an index finger. Instinctively, everyone inspected his genitals first, never to forget that time-honored story about a GI who found a leech partially up his penis. True or not, it's not the kind of story anyone with a penis is likely to forget. Anyway, a few troopers began ripping off the suckers and let the blood trickle. It was the quickest means of removal, but also the most painful and damaging to the skin. I had done it myself, but only when one or two locked onto my legs. This time, however, with so many leeches to remove, ripping them was not the best approach. Instead, troopers who smoked (many), and had steady hands (not so many), touched the lit end of their cigarettes to the aquatic worms and watched as they curled up and fell to the ground. Others, including me, squirted them with insect repellent. Leeches apparently didn't like bathing in it, and after a short wait, we could coax them off with our fingers. After helping each other remove leeches from our backsides, we inspected our fatigues for any hitchhikers before dressing.

I wore the same pungent, mud-caked fatigues for several more days until the front of my pants turned cardboard-like against my thighs. The constant chafing rubbed my skin raw until a dark ring about the size of a silver dollar appeared on my right thigh. The area was very tender to the touch. Doc said it was ringworm and gave me some kind of topical salve to put on it, along with directions to keep the area covered in gauze. A few applications of the salve and a clean change of fatigues did the trick; the painful ringworm faded away.

Captain Talbott routinely sent out protective flanks, especially when we traveled along recently used paths. With NVA and VC forces reportedly concentrating in our AO, we were less likely to fall prey to an enemy ambush when traveling in multiple formations. Along with sending out flanking units, the Old Man regularly split off additional platoons and squads on separate courses to cover more ground. Point men were discovering heavily used trails and booby traps, and nightly LPs were detecting more movement. Things were heating up all around us, and it didn't escape me that

I belonged to the same 7th Cavalry once led by Lieutenant Colonel George Armstrong Custer. Hopefully, that part of the 7th Cav's history would not repeat itself in Vietnam.

Late one morning, a small Cayuse observation helicopter known as a loach spotted four VC in the distance running through a field. As the "flying egg" and its three occupants approached to engage, the VC hid within tall elephant grass. The loach circled at low altitude over the original sighting but was not able to regain a visual. The pilot—probably a young warrant officer—requested foot soldiers to help flush out the VC. Alpha Company was the closest field unit in the area and so we got the assignment.

I could faintly hear rotor blades beating in the distance. Then a spurt of gunfire came from the same direction before the rotor blades stopped beating. Just then, battalion called. It said the pilot had put out a brief distress call before communication was lost. Concerned the loach had crashed, battalion ordered us to hurry to the site and secure the area. To save time, we pulled in our flanks and let point set a faster pace down a potentially booby-trapped path, putting him and others at greater risk.

In spite of the added danger, we arrived at the scene safely and discovered the downed loach, but not the crew. An aero squadron's rifle platoon, known as the Blues, had already flown in to evacuate the three occupants of the helicopter.

The loach was lying on its side with its tail section bent and its rotor blades twisted. The cockpit bubble was almost intact, which led me to think the crew had survived. But then I noticed blood in the cockpit and knew otherwise. On the ground nearby lay a crewman's helmet. Inside of it were bloody bits of bone and brain. The belly of the aircraft told the story: a line of bullet holes ran along the bottom decking. By the looks of it, the loach was hovering over the ground when a VC popped up and brought it down with a burst of automatic fire.

Charlie had likely *di di'd* (Vietnamese for move quickly) the area, but in case they were still hanging around, we fanned out through the tall grass. A second loach flew in to take up the search, joined this time by a Cobra attack helicopter. Working in tandem as a hunter-killer team, the highly maneuverable loach, or hunter, darted around at low altitude trying to spot the enemy. If successful, the co-pilot was ready to drop a smoke grenade before the pilot scooted away. Meanwhile, the deadly Cobra, or killer, circled far overhead watching for colored smoke. Catching sight of it, the Cobra would descend on the smoke firing its mini-guns and rockets, turning Charlie into Ground Chuck.

The loach was still flitting about when its occupants caught site of a VC running along a path. The rear passenger dispatched the lone runaway with his M-16 rifle. We regrouped and hurried up a path to offer assistance. Along the way, a grenade exploded at the head of the column. Yells for a medic followed. The lead RTO called saying our point man had tripped a wire strung across the path. Gilmore immediately got on the horn to summon a medevac as the captain led us up. When we arrived, medics were attending to two injured troopers. Both men had taken shrapnel, and both were in considerable pain. Squads fanned out to secure the area.

When the medevac landed full on the ground, a tracking team jumped out before we could load the wounded. Battalion had sent a handler and his trained dog (I think it was a black Labrador mix) to help flush out the VC and alert us to any more tripwires. By the time the tracking team took up point position and the handler gave his canine leash, the sun was dropping in the western sky. If the VC could remain undetected until dark, they could more easily slip away.

Within the hour, another grenade exploded up path. Again, the Old Man and his RTOs hurried forward. This time we found the handler and his dog bleeding on the ground. The Lab had failed to spot a tripwire and caught the brunt of the blast. It was lying on its side panting heavily and whimpering. The handler lay nearby, conscious and grimacing from non-life-threatening wounds. By the time the medevac picked them up, battalion decided to call off the search due to darkness, thus ending a highly frustrating day.

Alpha Company rotated back to Quoin Loi for some needed rest after a long stint in the field. Unfortunately, we didn't have time to enjoy it. Sometime before 14 November, lift birds flew 5th Battalion to Tay Ninh Province near the Cambodian border in an area known as the Fishhook. Our destination was LZ Jake, a small but well-established firebase located deeper inside Indian country. Defense of Jake fell upon a Montagnard civilian irregular defense group (CIDG, pronounced sidgee) and a detachment of the 5th Special Forces that provided training for the Montagnards.

Fifth Battalion established its forward headquarters at the LZ, adjacent to the special forces camp. Echo Company, or parts of it, joined headquarters, setting up its artillery pieces and mortar tubes. Battalion's four rifle companies, including Alpha, prepared a staging area downhill near a small airstrip and across a bridge that spanned a narrow point on the Saigon River. One rifle company dug in while the other three companies conducted operations inside War Zone C.

Several small fire support bases (FSBs) began popping up within the province to interdict communist infiltration toward Saigon. LZ Dot was one such firebase. It was located eight kilometers from the Cambodian border, and not far from LZ Jake. The U.S. 5th Artillery of the 1st Division's 1st Battalion was stationed there, along with units of the 36th ARVN Battalion. The communists took umbrage at the Cav's presence in the Fishhook and chose to make an example of Dot. On the night of 14 November, the LZ came under heavy attack from the 95th NVA Regiment, vastly outnumbering the allies at the firebase. The battle to overrun Dot raged throughout the night. Wave after wave of enemy soldiers tried to breach Dot's perimeter, and on more than one occasion they broke through. U.S. artillerymen from D Battery held off the charging waves, lowering their 105mm howitzer tubes and firing hundreds of rounds point-blank into their assailants. Howitzers on FSB Rita teamed with Jake's cannons to pound the area outside Dot's perimeter. Modified AC-47 fixed-wing aircraft called Spookys (also nicknamed Puff, the Magic Dragon, or Puff) entered the fray. They dropped illumination rounds to expose the NVA, and then strafed them with mini-guns that operated much like Gatling guns. Throughout the night, soldiers in the small perimeter blunted one attack after another.

At 0630H, the enemy broke contact. Within the hour, three rifle companies from 5th Battalion, including Alpha, air assaulted in to give chase. Cav slicks and gunships covered the sky around LZ Dot, surely a welcome sight to the exhausted soldiers there. Our three companies met only sporadic small-arms fire designed to slow our pursuit. This gave the NVA time to escape back into Cambodia, where our government forbade us to go. Within their safe haven, the communists could now refit without fear of reprisal and return to strike us another day. At least one company—Alpha—swept the area. Other units helped to re-establish perimeter defenses at Dot, and to collect the dead and wounded. The NVA lost a staggering 287 killed in action (KIA). ARVN loses stood at 9 KIA with 41 wounded in action (WIA), and 1 missing in action (MIA). U.S. casualties were only 7 WIA.

By the time Alpha Company walked back to LZ Dot late that afternoon, most of the dead and equipment were gone from the killing field. That night, we remained inside the perimeter in the event of another attack.

An RTO from a sister company sat up with me during a late radio watch. Looking up at the stars and the occasional illumination flare, we talked about the men on Dot. What they had accomplished was nothing short of extraordinary. They had repelled an all-night regimental onslaught, and in doing so, committed hundreds of enemy soldiers to the grave. This time last night, Dot was hell on earth. Tonight it was relatively quiet, and it would remain so by the time we left later in the morning.

Alpha Company operated in the field several more days before flying back to its staging area below LZ Jake. Upon our return, troopers took up the task of improving perimeter defenses. Gilmore and I helped fortify the CP bunker. We filled and stacked sandbags while Top issued instructions on how he wanted the bunker to look. At some point, Top left us alone and Gilmore decided he was the new straw boss. I wasn't surprised; he'd been treating me as his subordinate ever since my return to the company CP. But we were the same rank, and most of the time I just ignored him.

I used to wonder how Gilmore attained such a high level of self-importance. Maybe it was because he graduated from college and had earned a sheepskin, whereas the only sheepskin I ever possessed came from a bathroom vending machine. Neither had anything in common, really, other than both accommodated swelled heads. Maybe, too, he felt his age gave him higher status. He was, after all, a little older than me. Also, he probably felt cheated when the Army assigned him to a rifle company instead of a desk job at Cam Ranh Bay (a sentiment I could relate to). He even told me once how his college degree qualified him for a battlefield commission to 2nd lieutenant (oooh, aren't we full of ourselves). Anyway, his disdain wasn't limited to me, although I was probably at the top of his shit list. In my opinion, Gilmore merely tolerated most enlisted men at our rank or below because they couldn't further his ladder climbing. Instead he fawned over the three closest people to him who could best butter his bread: the CO, the XO, and Top. To get out of the field, Gilmore needed a fast-track promotion to battalion, and he knew I stood in the way. To even the odds, he tried to diminish me in front of our superiors to look more qualified. I was no match for Gilmore's brownnosing mastery. Instead, I concentrated on my job and hoped Captain Talbott would remember the commitment he made to me when I first came to his company.

So here we were filling sandbags, with Gilmore giving me directives, as if his supervision is important to the job. I finally told him to knock it off. He gave me some shit. I told him to eat some. So what's he do? He tells Top I'm not cooperating with the work at hand. And Top? He comes down on me without asking my side of the story. Score another one for Gilmore. The conniver knew how to spin the Top.

On 22 November, Alpha Company went UPCON (under operational control) to 2nd Battalion, 8th Cav. Our function was to temporarily increase the Cav's presence within the 2/8 area of operation where enemy activity was increasing.

As we prepared for another long stint in the bush, a French film crew received permission from 2nd Battalion to accompany us. Captain Talbott was not opposed to the idea, not that his opposition would have mattered, he just didn't want these nonmilitary types to get in our way. When he told the film crew to remain with the CP, one of the Frenchman nodded and smiled, but I think he was clueless to instruction (oui, oui, what time does ze train leave ze depot?).

By the time a sortie inserted our company into a small clearing, all RTOs had switched frequencies to match those of 2nd Battalion. The following day we exchanged fire with a small enemy force of unknown size, netting 1 NVA KIA and 0 U.S. casualties. The film crew waited until the shooting had stopped before taking advantage of their photo opportunity. Two days later we came across a line of commo wire strung along a trail. One end of the wire led to a recently occupied but now abandoned bunker complex. We inspected the site and then cautiously resumed our mission, discovering additional trails showing heavy use and more commo wire. Large, well-trained and well-armed NVA forces were out there somewhere. We could feel it. Our dogged pursuit kept tightening the noose; we just didn't know whose neck the noose was tightening around.

At the end of the day's hump, the photogs wandered away from the CP filming tired and edgy Skytroopers standing down. This was their final night in the field and they were taking full advantage of what little light remained. As for me, I was sitting on the ground heating a can of something over a small chunk of C-4 (taken from a claymore) when Gilmore walked up. He dictated my two radio shifts for the night and turned to leave. I called him back and pointed out how his rotation favored him again and suggested we change it. In an instant, Gilmore's face turned six shades of red. He leaned over me, clenched his teeth, and demanded I cooperate. Not intimidated, I told him to follow his own advice. Before I could react, Gilmore punched me hard on the face, rocking me backwards. Stunned by the blow, I could only watch the coward walk away. Those witnessing the incident looked amused. Captain Talbott, the XO, and Top Shaffer missed the assault, as they may have been with the film crew.

During my limited time in the field, I had endured every obstacle, withstood every humiliation, and tolerated every physical and emotional threat. But no more. Gilmore's punch, while it only cut my lip, impacted heavily on my state of mind. Up until now, I had successfully controlled building anger. But when his fist connected with my face, all that pent-up anger took control over my actions. Seething with rage and void of any self-control, I reached for my M-16. The bullying would end here and now. Gilmore would pay for his transgression. He would pay with his very life.

In measured steps, I walked toward my antagonist. He was sitting on a log talking with another grunt when they saw me approach. Their conversation abruptly stopped and uncertain looks came to their faces. When I reached them, in one smooth movement I deliberately pulled back the rifle's charging handle locking a round into the chamber. I flipped off the safety, brought the rifle butt to my shoulder, and pointed the muzzle between Gilmore's bugged eyes. When he saw my index finger curl around the trigger, he implored me not to shoot. I told him to shut up. Fortunately for the two of us, he obeyed my command.

By complying with my order, Gilmore essentially reversed our roles, putting me in the unfamiliar position of having control over him. And that's what ultimately saved his life, and my future. It was then I came to my senses and realized the consequences of my murderous intent.

Suddenly my overly confidant and controlling antagonist looked pitifully small at the end of my rifle barrel. I eased off the trigger, but with the weapon still poised, I said slowly and deliberately, "If you ever touch me again, I *will* kill you."

He just stared, frozen in place.

I lowered the rifle, and for effect, glared a moment longer into his saucer eyes. Then I walked away, but before taking my seat, I scanned the witnesses. Their expressions had changed from amusement to amazement, no doubt as a result of my uncharacteristic behavior. They quickly fell back into their routines and I sat down in shock, shaken to my core for coming so close to committing murder and cementing my destiny.

Gilmore didn't report me to the captain, and never again did he mention the incident. It would be the last time I had a significant problem with him, or anyone else in the company for that matter. It was as though I passed muster with the men for standing up for myself. For that they afforded me a measure of respect, despite my coming within a finger twitch of killing one of our own. It reminded me of the law of the jungle.

Had our visiting film crew remained embedded with our company the next day, 25 November, they could have captured some prize-worthy video. As it was, they left at dawn before our company moved out single file through heavy underbrush. First Platoon led the procession with Flip at point, even though it wasn't his turn. He volunteered to help a cherry unaccustomed to the nuances of the position. I think Flip liked the adrenaline rush of walking point, even with all the inherent dangers. He took chances with fate but he was not reckless, in my view. He simply was good at his job.

We had been humping well into the morning, slowed by oppressive heat and poor visibility, when the jungle suddenly erupted to our front. Thunderous bursts of AK-47 fire initiated return fire from our own riflemen and machine gunners. Multiple fragmentation grenades exploded from both sides. I dropped to the ground, barely able to hear my radio squeal from various RTOs hitting their send buttons at the same time. They were trying to either announce the obvious or ask for direction. Captain Talbott immediately grabbed Gilmore's handset to tell battalion that we were in heavy contact. Our FO checked his map and radioed Charlie Battery to alert them to a fire mission.

"Scarlet guidon 6-3, this is scarlet guidon 7-0, contact fire mission, over."

"Guidon 7-0, guidon 6-3, contact fire mission, out."

"6-3, 7-0, company in contact, grid x-ray alpha 123456, direction 2-3-0 degrees, enemy in bunkers, request delay fuse, battery 3 rounds in effect, will adjust, request splash, over."

"7-0, 6-3, roger, company in contact, enemy in bunkers, grid x-ray alpha 123456, direction 2-3-0 degrees, delay fuse, battery 3 rounds in effect, request splash, out." (Within thirty seconds, three rounds are shot.)

"7-0, 6-3, shot, over."

"6-3, 7-0, shot out."

"7-0, 6-3, splash, over." (Rounds will land in five seconds.)

"6-3, 7-0, right 100, drop 100, over."

"7-0, 6-3, right 100, drop 100, wait." (Pause.)

"7-0, 6-3, shot, over."

"6-3, 7-0, shot out."

"7-0, 6-3, splash, over."

"6-3, 7-0, splash out."

"6-3, 7-0, drop 30, fire for effect, over."

"7-0, 6-3, drop 30, fire for effect, wait."

"7-0, 6-3, shot, over."

"6-3, 7-0, shot out."

"7-0, 6-3, rounds complete, over."

"6-3, 7-0, rounds complete, out."

The NVA had dug in well, forcing our FO to advance the fire mission, making adjustments as needed.

Doc worked his way to the front while I responded to calls from platoon leaders wanting to speak to Line 6. I had to tell them to "hold one" until the Old Man finished with battalion. Captain Talbott finally took my handset and called 1-6, who detailed our situation. Lieutenant Fakler said his lead platoon walked into an NVA bunker complex with spider holes. The platoon was currently bogged down under intense fire. Troopers were trying to fan out to avoid LT's immediate concern, that of being outflanked. The CO took the information and ordered 2nd and 3rd Platoons to send out protective flanks and press the enemy. He then ordered 4th Platoon to move back to set up their mortar tubes and start clearing a small perimeter to take in a medevac. Top Shaffer went back to assist the fourth and to help care for the wounded as they arrived. Captain Talbott yelled "C'mon" to his RTOs and moved toward the front, holding the handsets tethered to our radios. Gilmore questioned the CO's decision to move closer to the action, telling him it might be better that he (referring to Talbott but meaning he, Gilmore) hang back. The CO paid no attention, whereas I quietly wished he had.

As the three of us crouch-walked toward the front line, twigs began sprinkling us from overhead. Initially puzzled by it, I soon realized that enemy bullets were snapping them off.

We continued forward, crawling now, until we stopped directly behind the battle line. From my new vantage point, the sheer volume of fire and sustained, ear-splitting noise were more fearsome and more deafening than anything I had ever known. My heart was pounding through my chest from a huge adrenaline rush. My senses were acute: colors were brighter, sounds were sharper, the smell of gunpowder hung in the air to where I could practically taste it. Never before had I felt more alive and yet so close to death.

Mortal combat has no emotional equal, in my opinion. The stress of such an event is that great. I don't think any soldier can assume to know how he will react in battle until he first experiences it. It was certainly true in my case. During the initial phase of battle, I did fairly well staying on task, as I had expected. But it wasn't long before I reached sensory overload and zoned out. I lapsed into a hypnotic fog, shamelessly oblivious to everything around me, including important calls coming in over my radio. Luckily, Captain Talbott did hear the calls. He snatched away the handset and gave me a quick shove. Fortunate for the company he did. That was all I needed to get back into the game.

The call he took was from Davy Miller saying Lieutenant Fakler was hit. It occurred when LT and an enemy soldier took cover on opposite sides of a large anthill. Staying low to the ground, LT reached over the anthill with his M-16 and began spraying bullets on the opposite side. When his magazine emptied, he started to crawl away when an enemy frag tumbled down his side of the anthill. It exploded, ripping into LT's shoulder and hand. Davy said LT was ambulatory, but that he was in no shape to lead the platoon. Captain Talbott told Davy to put Sergeant Carter in charge and have the lieutenant meet us at our position. Being only steps away, LT and Davy soon emerged from the underbrush. My former platoon leader had his bloodied left hand elevated near his bloodied left shoulder. Streaks of red ran down his forearm. He acted disoriented, even smiled inappropriately to conditions on the ground. Talbott had someone escort LT back to the medical evacuation area and sent Davy up to Sergeant Carter.

Heavy fighting continued to our front. Troopers began reporting sporadic fire on our flanks. Captain Talbott reacted quickly, telling the FO to walk cannon rounds closer to our position—a dangerous maneuver but a necessary one if we hoped to thwart the enemy. He then alerted all platoons to the impending close support.

Our FO adjusted fire data with redleg before yelling over the radio "Fire for effect!" In the meantime, the battalion commander called us. He said F-4 Phantom jets were on the way to provide close air support and for us to prepare to pull back when they came on station.

All this time I had been sitting with my legs crossed, taking calls, when I took a sharp blow to my right hand. I yelled out in pain and looked down to see blood dripping from between my thumb and forefinger. My first thought was, *I've been shot!* Lying on the ground next to me was a jagged chunk of metal about the size of a man's fist. Without thinking, I picked it up with my left hand. The metal instantly burned my fingertips. I yelled out again and dropped the fragment. While I looked at my blistering fingers, my penis felt like it had come in contact with a hot iron. Without realizing it, I had dropped the searing lead on my lap, where it was now scorching the crotch of my pants. I yelled out for a third time and spun to my side, letting the fragment slide to the ground. Captain Talbott heard all the yelling and turned to see my bloodied hand. "You been shot?"

"No," I said, pointing to the chunk of metal. "Shrapnel from arty."

"You got yourself a Purple Heart, Hoffmann" he declared, and then ordered the FO to push back the cannon rounds. I took out my olive drab handkerchief and wrapped it around the wound. This was no time to consider getting a Purple Heart when under these conditions it could still be awarded posthumously.

By the time the Navy's F-4s came on station, artillery bombardments had blunted enemy flanking maneuvers. Our FO switched gears and directed the fighter pilots to the bunker complex while Captain Talbott radioed his rifle platoon leaders to pull back. Sergeant Carter balked at the directive. He wanted more time to reach his downed point man. His statement only confirmed my suspicion that Flip was dead or wounded. Talbott denied Carter's request, ordering him to pull back immediately. Our company needed to *di di* before the jets started dropping their bombs.

Those of us in the CP waited for all troopers to file behind us. Sergeant Carter was the last to appear. At that point, no one came between the CP and the enemy. We had now become the new front line. The six of us—Talbott, his two RTOs, the XO, the FO and his RTO—were now facing the bunker complex. The Old Man yelled to us, "Expect the gooks to follow from their bunkers. Lay down fire! Let's go! Let's go!"

The six of us walked backwards, spraying the bushes with short bursts of automatic fire. I held my weapon tight under my arm and spit out three rounds with each squeeze of the trigger. The captain and the XO were in front of me and to either side. I had to be careful not to sweep the muzzle too far left or right. A small deviation in either direction would have turned them into friendly-fire casualties. Everyone else was firing his weapon from behind me, including Gilmore. He was shooting so close to my torso that he could have easily rendered some serious payback, and would have probably gotten away with it.

When arty announced "tubes clear," the first jet abruptly appeared from behind and to my right. It screamed over the treetops, so close that I could actually see the pilot sitting in the cockpit. The jet released two high explosive bombs before nosing up sharply. From the direction of the bunker complex came two loud explosions followed by clouds of smoke. Captain Talbott yelled for everyone to hightail it. As the command post turned back up path, he continued walking backwards firing his weapon. He wasn't alone. I stepped up next to him and side by side, we emptied one magazine after another into the tangled underbrush.

"C'mon!" The Old Man yelled to me before he turned away. Why I don't know, but at that moment I felt more aggressive than scared, and I was plenty scared. I continued walking backwards pulling at the trigger while challenging those dirty sons-a-bitches to follow if they dared. When my next magazine emptied, I took off behind the captain until we reached 4th Platoon's defensive position.

CP personnel collected around Top. He said one medevac had made it in to pick up the wounded, including Lieutenant Fakler. On the ground next to us lay a dead rifleman who had suffocated in his own blood after an AK round shattered his jaw. Someone came over and put a poncho over him, covering all but his lifeless feet. I fixed my eyes on the dead soldier's boots and irrationally wished him to get up. Then I looked at the bloody handkerchief covering my hand. I removed it and rinsed the wound with water finding two minor cuts, one of which had nicked a vein. The differences between my cut hand and the solder's shattered jaw were obvious. My wounds were insignificant by comparison, hardly worthy of a Purple Heart.

One by one, the F-4 Phantoms skimmed over the treetops dropping their ordnance. Some bombs tumbled end over end and made only muffled noises on impact. Billowing black clouds rose over the trees, a telltale sign they were burning napalm, ostensibly incinerating the NVA into "crispy critters."

Dusk was fast approaching and we needed to put distance between the bunker complex and our company. Fighter jets were providing the diversion we needed to withdraw. We gathered our dead and moved as far as daylight would allow—probably not more than a klick or two away—before stopping to set up a night defensive perimeter. Everybody dug in. Later, battalion called to say Delta Company 2/8 had been working toward our position, but they had stopped for the night a few klicks away. I liked knowing friendlies were out there somewhere.

After dark, the Old Man gathered his platoon leaders and said we would not abandon our dead trooper. At first light the company was going back in to retrieve Flip. He suspected any survivors of the bombing would have fled by morning. It was an assumption not without risk—a risk we were willing to take.

L to R Tom Berkfield (KIA 12/9/1968), Davy Miller,
Gary "Flip" Throckmorton (KIA 11/25/1968)

Events of the day kept me awake into the night. Men on perimeter, and especially those on LP, may have fared no better. I dwelled on the day's fight and my dumb-ass decision to be the last man out in the face of gunfire. What possessed me to do such a crazy thing? Was it to show the captain that I had the guts I'd not shown him earlier when I froze in battle? Or to show myself, possibly? Maybe I did it because the Old Man was standing alone and I felt obligated to support him. I'd like to think that. Or maybe I suffered from temporary insanity, who knows. Whatever the impetus, I needed to cut that shit out if I expected to get home alive and in one piece. Let others demonstrate their bravery, or foolishness, or however one looks at it. Use your head, man, I said to myself.

Too often, though, emotion trumps logic, as it had in this case. All the while I was getting down on myself, I was at the same time feeling self-pride for doing what was for me, this ordinary draftee, something extraordinary. It felt good, in a troubling sort of way.

When sunlight peeked over the horizon, our camp began to stir. I cracked open an eyelid and cursed the morning. My body felt paralyzed from fatigue and my right hand throbbed, but I didn't have the energy to raise it for inspection.

All was so peaceful....

Poomp. The sound came from outside the perimeter—a mortar round leaving its tube.

Delta Company? I wondered. They that close? *BOOM.* The round exploded near camp.

That ain't Delta!

Another *poomp*, followed this time by yells of incoming. My previously unresponsive body miraculously came to life. With the moves of a gazelle, I grabbed my steel pot, M-16, boots and socks, and rolled into my pitiful foxhole. Another explosion. Closer still, but not too close.

Poomp. I pictured the mortar round arching into the sky and gravity hurling it back to earth. The queasy question was, where on earth? In the precious few seconds before impact, I threw on my socks. *BOOM.* Charlie's aim was getting better, but his rounds were still exploding at a harmless distance. Or maybe not—our LPs could still be out there somewhere. I looked toward the radios. Someone was manning them. *Good.*

Poomp. I threw on my boots and raced to the radios without lacing them. The FO was there. He had already given preset DTs to arty. *BOOM.* Another errant round. *Fucking rookies.*

From outside our perimeter came a much larger explosion. One of ours. Maybe a dime-nickel (105mm howitzer) shell. Artillery brought the desired effect. Mortar fire ceased and calm returned, as did the LPs, unscathed.

When I finished cinching my ruck, I removed the bandage from my wounded hand to have a look. The bleeding had stopped long ago and the swelling was down, but the soreness had increased around my trigger finger and thumb. I decided not to re-bandage the wound and let it air out.

Everyone understood the risks of returning to yesterday's battle site. We also knew it had to be done. Radio operators switched off their speakers and kept a sharp ear to their handsets. Second Platoon got lead assignment, with Sergeant Pat Smith's squad taking point.

Alpha moved cautiously through the heavy underbrush. Along the way, I bumped my wounded hand on something and reopened the vein. A slight trickle of blood ran down my thumb and forefinger. There was no time to deal with it, so I let the blood crust over.

Sergeant Smith calls me. They have just spotted a gook lookout jumping from a distant tree. Captain Talbott considers the troubling news. He knows the lookout is there to warn the survivors of yesterday's bombing. The issue becomes, how many will he warn and what will they do? Will they hunker down for another protracted fight, or will they cut and run like we expect. Sergeant Smith receives his orders. We forge ahead.

Farther along the way, I get another call. Point is nearing the bunkers. Tense minutes pass. Another call. Sergeant Smith whispers he has a visual on Flip's body, but no gooks. I'm not surprised. They'd be stupid to face more bombing, more shelling, and more ground forces. The squad moves forward to collect Flip's remains. Another minute passes. Everyone is waiting nervously for the call to say mission complete. But when it comes, Smith says they are pulling back; the body is booby-trapped with one of our own claymore mines. *BOOM.* The claymore explodes. AKs, 16s and 60s erupt. Grenades explode. It is heart-pounding chaos all over again.

Battalion orders Captain Talbott to make a tactical withdrawal (*retreat* when referring to the enemy). We must do so in advance of more bombings, including a B-52 bomber air strike scheduled later that night.

Eventually—I say eventually because time was a blur—our company was able to break contact and pull back to an area where the wounded could be evacuated. For all our efforts and good intentions, we ended up with additional wounded, and with Flip's body still unrecovered.

Supporting cannon fire paused long enough to let a medevac from the 15th Medical Battalion attempt a pickup. The gutsy flight crew and medical personnel swooped in to land full on the ground. Painted on the slick's nose was the International Red Cross logo.

Helped aboard the aircraft were Algire, Chess, Ebel, Perkins, Piconi, Tex Rainer, Sergeant Smith, and the body of Sergeant Brix. Once fully loaded, the medevac labored off the ground. Tex was sitting at the edge of the door holding his blood-soaked arm. We gave a thumbs up and Tex responded in kind, flashing us a confident smile until they disappeared from sight.

Battalion instructed us to hump at least three kilometers from the bunker complex and dig foxholes in advance of an Arc Light mission. Sometime overnight, B-52 Stratofortress bombers would fly over the bunkers at an altitude of up to 30,000 feet and drop 500- to 750-pound bombs on the NVA stronghold, turning bunkers into graves. Those potent bombs had a wide kill zone. They also could inflict terrible injuries outside the immediate kill zone, injuries like brain trauma, internal organ hemorrhaging, bleeding from the nose and ears, and disorientation. At the very least, they would strike terror in anyone who experienced a close encounter. That's why battalion ordered our company to withdraw three klicks, the minimum prescribed distance from ground zero.

Weary troopers pushed through the steamy underbrush for less than three klicks when the order came to set up a perimeter. Everyone dug in and tried to rest. After dark, CP personnel huddled together anticipating a call from battalion. We expected to get our marching orders for the next day and a medical report on the wounded flown out earlier. When the call came, 2nd Battalion's lieutenant colonel asked for County Line 6 over my speakerphone. Captain Talbott got on the horn while the CP listened to the conversation.

The battalion CO started out by saying he had bad news to report and then paused to let his words sink in. That seemed odd. Ranking officers usually came right out with their bad news. In a glum voice, he said the medevac carrying out our wounded was intercepted by enemy 50-caliber ground fire. The helicopter went down. All passengers and crew died in the crash.

A pall fell over the CP. Everyone sat in stunned silence as the battalion CO continued his report. He said an Aero Blue team recovered the bodies, including that of a soldier identified as Rainer, whom they found several meters from the crash scene. The Blues suspected Rainer had jumped prior to impact in a vain attempt to save himself. The battalion commander expressed his sorrow for our losses and thanked us for a job well done. He ended by telling Captain Talbott to have our company ready in the morning for an airlift back to LZ Jake. At that point, 5th Battalion would assume operational control.

Drooping his head, Captain Talbott let the handset drop to the ground. No one spoke. During the silence, I tried to accept the reality of the moment, but it was hard to comprehend the sudden deaths of all those men. With clarity, I could still picture Tex sitting at the edge of the helicopter as it labored off the ground. Hurting from his wounds, he still had the presence of mind to flash us a confident thumbs up as a way of saying everything would be all right. And there we were, returning the gesture as he and the others faded from sight. Forever faded from sight.

I had another reality to work through; it was that I almost rode on that same doomed flight. Right after the medevac landed to make the pickup, I asked Captain Talbott if I should board with the other wounded. I displayed the dried blood on my hand and told him it hurt like hell. The Old Man said he didn't like the idea of losing his RTO, and particularly under our circumstances. But because he didn't know if my hand was broken—and I purposely didn't tell him it wasn't—he authorized me to board, but only after the more seriously wounded were loaded. I'm ashamed by this admission, but there it is.

Obviously, I never boarded the medevac. During the time it took to load the wounded, I grew balls. I retracted my request and stood with the captain while troopers helped load the wounded and the body of Sergeant Brix, a spot I possibly could have taken.

When Captain Talbott regained his composure that evening, he called in his lieutenants to discuss matters of the day. Later, everyone retired under the cover of darkness to deal privately with his thoughts.

Sometime after midnight, the world came crashing in around us from a series of thunderous, ear-splitting explosions. The sky lit up, and the ground shook so violently that I literally bounced off it. The hell of it was, there was no place to run or hide. All anyone could do was to ride out the B-52 air strike and hope for the best.

When the bombing paused, the Old Man got on the horn and yelled for battalion to call off the Arc Light, but he could've saved his breath; the mission had already ended. I called for a company-wide sitrep and learned everyone came through the ordeal pretty shook up but otherwise unhurt. Those big bombs exploded dangerously close to our position, which made us wonder if any hit their intended target.

Just after dawn, Cobra gunships circled overhead to guard a sortie of slicks as they came in for the pickup. I took a seat in exactly the same position Tex was sitting in during his ill-fated flight. While skimming over the treetops, I envisioned large 50-caliber rounds blowing holes through the floor plate, ripping through metal and flesh. I looked down at the trees and tried to picture Tex pushing out of the slick in his desperate but suicidal attempt to survive impact. It was completely unnerving to me, and its effects would be long lasting. From that day forward, I felt more vulnerable riding in helicopters. And on at least one occasion, I thought we were going to crash when our slick was simply dropping to treetop level before landing.

Slicks off-loaded Alpha Company at the end of LZ Jake's runway. From there, we crossed the bridge to our camp, which was also near the Montagnard compound. We could now rest for the next few days.

While we settled in, a doctor rode down in a jeep to tend to the slightly injured. He asked us to fill out note cards with our personal information, along with the nature of our wounds. My cuts were so minor that I thought about not filling out a card, and probably would not have but for Captain Talbott's indelible words, "Hoffmann, you got yourself a Purple Heart." So I filled out a card and then stood with a handful of other soldiers who had wounds no worse than mine, or so it seemed. When my turn came, the doctor took my card, examined my hand and found that the wounds were healing well on their own. He gave me a tetanus shot, some bandages, and sent me along.

It is now two days later, 28 November, Thanksgiving Day, and I could give a flying fig about the holiday. If there was anything to be thankful for, it was for the news we received that the B-52's had destroyed the bunker complex, and a recovery team had collected Flip's remains. My thoughts went out to the dead soldiers' families, and I wondered if the Army had yet notified them. If yes, this day of giving thanks would surely be lost in their grief. I also pictured my own family and relatives back home. They would be gathering around our holiday dinner table eating Mom's notoriously dry turkey. I hoped they were thinking of me as much as I was thinking of them.

That afternoon, our company received a traditional Thanksgiving dinner of warm turkey with all the fixings. Servers from LZ Jake brought the meals down in metal cans and rationed out the food on metal trays. It was a fine feast, for sure.

During chow, a C-130 cargo plane approached the far end of the small airstrip. It landed long and braked hard, but it couldn't stop before skidding off the runway. The front landing gear broke off in the ground, turning the nosecone into a plow. The aircraft came to an abrupt stop moments before the side door flew open and crewmen jumped out. Some of our guys ran to offer assistance, while others grabbed their cameras. No one was hurt that I remember.

A reference to the C-130 incident and downed medevac can be found in a *Chicago Tribune Magazine* article from 24 January 1969. Mom sent me the piece not knowing it had any relevance to my situation. She knew only that it was about the 1st Cav. Written by Ridgley Hunt and titled "Combat Assault," the article quotes Mowdy, a chopper pilot, and Grannemann, an operations officer.

> "'Once you take off out of the PZ,'" said Grannemann, "it's all Indian country. There are no friendlies. If you get shot at, you have full authority to shoot back in this area," he said, pointing to the map. "We've been having heavy .50 caliber fire. We had a medevac shot down here with all 12 aboard killed. We have three MIA's" – missing in action – "in the area and we want you to pick them up." (Bring back their bodies, he means.)
>
> "Do we have any known enemy positions?" Mowdy asked.
>
> "The whole thing is enemy positions," Grannemann replied.
>
> On the map, (Mowdy) showed the (pilots) where they would go the next morning and discussed the prep, which this time included B-52 bombing.
>
> "In case you haven't seen it," another aviator said, "they got a C-130 down off the end of the runway at LZ Jake.'"

I also made reference to the firefights in a letter I sent Ron after my promotion to battalion. In it, my resentment toward the enemy is clearly evident.

> ...you probably heard about what happened over here. Two days before Thanksgiving our company got into a big firefight with those little slant-eyed bastards. When all was over, we had 10 killed and 5 wounded and I got a Purple Heart. Nothing serious, just a little shrapnel to my hand. After all that, battalion pulled me out of the field finally and made me one of the colonel's RTO's.

Sunday, the battalion chaplain and other officers came down to attend memorial services for the dead. The scene was reminiscent of pictures I had seen honoring soldiers killed in combat. A rifle fixed with bayonet represented each fallen soldier. Rifles were stuck vertically in the ground by their bayonets and lined up in formation. A steel pot lay on top of each rifle stock and a pair of boots stood below. The service was very somber. Some men showed their emotions during the ceremony. Others, like me, bore witness in numbed silence.

Afterward, I was resting alone under my staked poncho when Captain Talbott lifted a corner and asked, "You ready to move up to battalion?"

I couldn't believe my ears. Was this the moment I thought might never come? No more humping a radio; no more wet nights in the bush; no more search and destroy; no more Gilmore? All I needed to do was utter two simple words: "Yes" and "sir." But I couldn't say them. And this from a guy who would have given his left nut (and almost did) to get out of the field. Instead, I asked, "Are you okay with this?"

Captain Talbott was taken aback. "Isn't that what you want? What you trained for?"

I finally came to my senses. "Yes, sir, I *am* ready to move up."

The Old Man told me to collect my personal gear and report to the tactical operations center at LZ Jake. And then, as he stood to leave, he paused. "Good luck, Hoffmann, I'll say goodbye to the men for you."

"Thank you, sir, and good luck to all of you."

And with that I threw together my stuff, walked across the bridge and up the dirt road leaving my company behind.

This wasn't how I envisioned the moment to be. Not by a long shot. For starters, I had no hint of it coming. Also, any joy and excitement I had come to expect was peculiarly absent. I felt like I was abandoning my company and my responsibilities to the men. It was all very weird to think I had developed an unlikely bond with my fellow Skytroopers over the course of our contentious three months. But as I continued to walk up the hill, I understood my reluctance to leave them. Foot soldiers can form emotional attachments when they live together, fight together, bicker, laugh, grieve and suffer together. They become a family, of sorts. And that's why I felt guilty for leaving them now. It can be a heavy guilt not easily overcome.

So, did I get over it? You bet your sweet ass, and before the day was out.

Battalion RTO

O nce inside LZ Jake's perimeter, I was surprised to see several Vietnamese women and children milling about. This was, after all, a front-line military outpost, so what in the world were civilians doing here? It turned out they were the families of Montagnard men who provided defense of the camp they called Tong Le Chon, or Tonle Cham. Montagnards were a minority mountain people who lived in simple societies. Some of the women walked in the open unabashedly bare breasted. The smallest children were naked, potbellied, and cute. I watched as they helped their more modestly dressed older siblings police the dirt for discarded cigarette butts to smoke.

Montagnard men serving in the military liked their bush hats and tight-fitting, tiger-striped utilities that accentuated their uniformly diminutive bodies. Responsibility for their training came from a contingent of 5th Special Forces. The SF camp was adjacent to 5th Battalion's forward headquarters and tactical operations center, currently housed in a tent. Nearby, a more substantial TOC was in the final stages of construction. The box-shaped structure was completely aboveground. The walls and ceiling were made from some kind of steel-coated planking designed for what original purpose, I don't know. When I arrived, soldiers were busy filling sandbags and stacking them against the walls.

Nearby, two men were sitting on chairs under a plastic canopy to escape the sun. They were manning a bank of radios I recognized as PRC-25s and PRC-47s. The radios were connected to tall, omni-directional mast antennas guy-wired to the ground. I assumed correctly they were 5th Battalion RTOs and introduced myself as their new radio operator. Tim and Lane immediately put me at ease with their handshakes and smiles. Although I had never seen them before, their voices were familiar; I had spoken with them many times over the radio. Lane in particular had a distinctive baritone voice with an air of authority to it. It was a fitting voice for a guy who always sounded cool under pressure, even when field companies were in the middle of chaotic firefights.

I talked with both men for probably longer than I should have, but curiosity about their jobs got the better of me. I kept asking questions and they kept answering, including how I was likely to be one of their replacements since they both were short-timers. When I finally got around to asking where to report, they identified a nearby tent as the temporary TOC.

Standing in front of the tent was an officer of major rank. I reported and he returned my salute pro forma. Major Dalton welcomed me to 5th Battalion's headquarters and said he looked forward to working with me as the battalion's S-3 operations officer. After some small talk, he had me report to the communications officer who was inside the tent. It was there I received another warm greeting from my section chief, Captain Blair. Everyone was so relaxed and approachable that I began to feel downright coddled. And it would only get better.

We chatted a while before he led me to my living quarters not far from the TOC. The billet was a large, rectangular-shaped canvas wall tent. The sides were rolled up to release trapped heat, and sandbags—stacked to a height of about three feet— surrounded the tent. Inside, maybe eighteen or so cots lined the dirt floor along opposite sides. Made of canvas and wood, the cots came with air mattresses and mosquito netting. Captain Blair pointed to the third cot on the right and said to stow my gear under it. I was practically giddy at the thought of sleeping off the ground and under roof.

Battalion's other two radio operators happened to be in the tent, completing the team of four. Introductions weren't necessary, as it turned out. One of the two men was Digger. He was the guy who spent a night in the field with us when Lieutenant Colonel McGraw came to visit. The other guy had attended my radio course at Fort Huachuca several months earlier. Back then Larry wore a black armband with corporal stripes sewn to it, signifying his status as a temporary platoon leader. He was an intelligent, fair-minded trainee leader who showed no favoritism, even to his black brothers at Huachuca who saw him as somewhat of an outsider.

"Sergeant Hoffmann, it's you," he said, extending his hand.

"Sorry to say you're only half right. I'm back to my authorized rank of Spec 4 again. And call me Phil."

Captain Blair interrupted our conversation to say the three of us could continue talking while filling sandbags at the new TOC. The other work crew needed a break, he said. Digger and Larry groaned at the prospect of physical labor, while I could only smile. Compared to humping the bush, shoveling sand into woven plastic bags and stacking them under a hot sun would be akin to playing in a sandbox.

In a few days our new headquarters was ready to occupy. Work crews had finished stacking sandbags around the outside walls. Fill dirt was then dumped over the sandbags and tapered to about a 45-degree angle to the ground. Sand-filled ammo boxes were used to form the entrance. They were stacked and designed in the shape of an S to protect the interior from flying shrapnel.

Positioned immediately inside the entrance was redleg's communications desk. To the left of redleg, a larger table fit snugly against the opposite wall. A bank of radios lined that table, and all were reserved for battalion radio operators. One radio was designated a backup for the others. The rest performed specific functions on separate frequencies. The PRC-47 radios were larger and more powerful than the portable PRC-25 I carried in the field. One handled communications within our 5th Battalion net. Key it up and all five companies would get the call. Another provided commo between individual companies. The frequency on that radio changed depending on the company it was to reach. Two more PRC-47s handled commo between battalion and 3rd Brigade HQ. One of them encrypted and decrypted voice modulation designed to handle sensitive or classified information. Operating secure radios was no different from operating unsecured radios, except when someone pushed the send button on a secure radio, he had to wait for a beep before speaking. The beep meant his voice was being scrambled over the airwaves until the receiving radio, also secure, unscrambled it. The trouble with these sophisticated transmitter/receivers was that they often failed.

To the right of our commo room was the strategy/map room. Behind it were the sleeping quarters for Lieutenant Colonel McGraw and his S-3 operations officer. The colonel's executive officer spent most of his time at Quan Loi with 5th Battalion rear.

During my first few days at LZ Jake, I worked alongside Lane learning the ropes. Due to his capable guidance and my prior experience, I quickly fell into a comfortable groove working the radios. Finally, I was in my element, my comfort zone.

Aside from the obvious similarities between battalion and company radio operations, such as push to talk and release to listen, there were plenty of differences between the two jobs. While in the field, I was responsible for my prick-25 all my waking hours. At battalion, a staff of radio operators (generally four) worked a bank of radios in single shifts. That is to say, each of us worked at least one six-hour shift within a twenty-four hour period, seven days a week. We also worked in teams, especially when radio traffic was heavy. And then there were those double shifts when someone took R & R (rest and recreation). Still, I had far more free time here than I had in the field, although the job had its own pressures.

Battalion RTOs were under the microscope from many high-ranking officers, who often funneled their radio communications through us. Lieutenant Colonel McGraw was the most intimidating of any. He would bark orders to his RTOs to pass on lengthy, sometimes confusing messages. "No, dammit, I told you to tell him [blah blah]," before he'd grab the handset from our hands and finish the call himself. Or when he didn't like the answer coming from one of his junior officers in the field, he'd yank away the handset and unabashedly dress down the officer. That was always my cue to stand clear, for the colonel had a bad habit of throwing down the handset. But we soon learned he was more bark than bite. For all his gruffness, he cared deeply for his men. You could see it in his face when we took casualties.

In addition to giving, taking, or relaying messages between five companies and brigade, battalion RTOs performed routine communications. We requested sitreps with companies in the field and noted their positions several times a day. New to me at battalion was my responsibility to maintain written logs, something company RTOs were not required to do. Any logged information had to include the date, time, unit name, and the message or description of the event. Each morning our S-3 collected the previous day's logs and transferred the data onto another form. These logs were slated for archive after the war as part of the 1st Cavalry's unit history. Examples are in this book.

One person not often seen in the TOC was our ranking NCO, a command sergeant major. Word had it he and the colonel didn't get along very well, so command sergeant major generally avoided the company's nerve center.

When I finally got my own shift, it was the 2200H to 0400H time slot, pretty much SOP for any new radio operator. No one relished the late shift, but as the new guy, I liked it. It was a good way to become acclimated within my new environs and to gain confidence with fewer people looking over my shoulder. Officers would be in bed and field companies would be retired inside their night defensive positions. With few exceptions, radio traffic was lighter at night than during the day. The hardest part about working the late shift was dealing with boredom. There were times I'd get sleepy listening to the drone of the outside generator and the incessant white noise from the radio's speakers. Good that redleg was sitting across the room so we could help each other stay awake.

At least once every hour I got to use my new call sign to initiate a company-wide sitrep. I'd say into the handset: "Fast Flanker niner-niner, Flanker 6-5, request sitreps, over." Alpha Company was always first in line to respond, and depending on his shift, Gilmore sometimes answered my call. I swear I could detect resentment in his voice, especially on those stormy nights in the field. He'd be all wet and miserable, and I'd be all dry and cozy. *Nightie-night, Gilmore.*

Sleep tight. Don't let the bedbugs bite. After company sitreps, I'd wait for brigade to call for battalion sitreps.

Mark, the redleg RTO who worked the desk behind me, was good company, at least for a while. Late one night I asked him if he would take a picture of me sitting at my table. I wanted to send the print home to my parents as proof that I was out of the field. After lining up all the handsets on the table, I held one to my ear and said, "Ready." Mark pushed the button and a flash lit up the TOC. Then came another flash, but it wasn't from the camera. Lieutenant Colonel McGraw bolted like a flash out of his room and demanded to know what the hell was going on. Mark quickly explained that he was only taking a picture of me sitting at the table, but the colonel was not appeased. He railed about having classified documents in the room and threatened to confiscate the roll of film. I jumped in and said my only intention was to show my parents where I worked, and that classified documents and maps were not in the picture. The Old Man eventually calmed down and retired to his room without destroying the film, but he ordered no more pictures taken inside his TOC.

As more nights passed, Mark's personality gradually changed. He became more withdrawn. It happened slowly at first. Each night he would get a little more moody, a little more remote. I had no idea what was causing his anti-social behavior, but I knew he'd been working a string of double shifts while redleg was short of operators. On what turned out to be his last shift at radio, I asked him early on if I had said or done something to piss him off. "No," was his only reply. Late that same morning, about shift change, Mark got a call. He didn't answer it. "It's yours, man," I said, turning to see him only stare at the radio. I walked over and took the call at about the same time his replacement came in. When the guy asked for the chair, Mark didn't respond.

The whole business was starting to creep me out, and so I asked Mark's replacement to summon Captain Blair. Soon our sleepy communications chief entered the TOC and asked his RTO to get up. Mark didn't comply, nor did he answer. He remained seated, staring intensely at the radio. Clearly surprised by the insubordination, Captain Blair turned his request into an order, and he did so with emphasis. "Specialist, as your superior officer I am ordering you to get up!" Mark continued to stare at the radio. With tears welling up in his eyes, he blurted out, "Can't leave my post."

By now Captain Blair must have suspected he was dealing with a fruit-loop. Taking a softer approach, he took Mark gently by the arm and quietly encouraged him to get up. Mark yanked free his arm, and with tears now running down his face, he yelled, "NO!" Thoroughly frustrated by his lack of persuasive powers, Captain Blair followed the only course of action left to him: brute force. He nodded to Mark's replacement and the two men grabbed him under each arm and tried to lift him off the chair. That provoked Mark into a violent, crying rage. I had to jump into the fray to help restrain the lunatic. Finally Mark went limp. Later, we led the broken shell of a man out the door and into a waiting helicopter that took him away. We never saw the poor bastard again.

My guess is the Army performed a medical evaluation on Mark and sent him home, maybe even discharged him. I'm also guessing that once he left the Army, our government offered him little in the way of extended psychological counseling. From what I understand, the military was better adapted to treat physical trauma than it was psychological trauma. Returning Vietnam vets who needed extended counseling generally didn't get it, or ask for it. Our government was more likely to release them into their communities, where many had trouble assimilating back into a social order. It wasn't until the mid-1980s that the U.S. Department of Veteran Affairs officially recognized the trauma as post-traumatic stress disorder, or PTSD. The VA eventually extended benefits to the afflicted, but it came too late for a multitude of war veterans who had already lost their marriages, their physical health, and their ability to hold down meaningful jobs due to PTSD. That's what happened to a good friend of mine who I've known since grade school. He has PTSD, and he has allowed me to share his story.

The Army drafted Jerry in 1968 and sent him to Cu Chi, South Vietnam. He was assigned to the 25th Division's 25th Medical

Detachment. An RTO by training (I was his instructor at Fort Huachuca), Jerry facilitated medical evacuations between ground forces and dustoff crews (dustoff is another term for medevac). While on base, he got to know crewmen who told him stories about their work. Impressed by their harrowing rescues of injured soldiers on the battlefield, Jerry wanted to do more than operate a radio behind a desk and asked if he could fly with them during his off hours. The crewmen were impressed, and so they authorized him to ride under the status of patient protector.

Jerry rode on many dustoff missions offering support to the wounded. He proved so capable that a flight commander once wrote of him: "Specialist Gebhardt's actions played a critical role in the successful evacuation of many battlefield casualties."

But witnessing death and dealing with danger on a regular basis took a toll on my friend. On what would be his last dustoff flight, a crewman asked if he would come along on a critical night extraction. Jerry had only enough time to jump on board without first retrieving his rifle. In flight, he learned their pickup was near Nui Ba Din, the Black Virgin Mountain, one of the most dangerous pickup zones in their area, and especially at night. Without his rifle for protection, he began to experience an escalating sense of foreboding. By the time the dustoff reached the mountain and began negotiating a risky landing, Jerry convinced himself the chopper was going to crash from enemy gunfire. He also believed he would survive impact, but without his M-16, he knew the enemy would capture, torture, and kill him. As he expressed it to me, his body felt like it was "decomposing." He completely zoned out and became totally oblivious to outside stimuli. The next thing he remembered was a crewman shaking him, saying, "Jerry, we're back." It was only then he realized the helicopter was sitting on the landing pad at Tay Ninh and that the wounded had already off-loaded. Having lost touch with time and reality, he got off the Huey and walked away without speaking to the crew. A couple days later, the Red Cross summoned my friend home on a medical emergency, not for him but for his father, who was involved in a serious auto accident.

Jerry remained stateside for the remainder of his military obligation to help care for his father. He got a job, paid taxes, and married. He also began to drink heavily and had issues with anger he could not manage. Not able to control his inner demons, he eventually lost his job and his marriage. Many years elapsed before Jerry got help through the VA. Group counseling with other PTSD veterans helped him recall for the first time since Vietnam that last dustoff mission when his mind went to black. His healing process continues and I'm happy to say that I got my fun-loving buddy back.

While Jerry continues to heal, there are many other less fortunate war veterans who find themselves homeless and addicted within the septic bowels of our cities. These are patriots who fought America's wars during our time of need and who today suffer from service-related illnesses. Our country should do no less than fight for them during their time of need.

Who knows, maybe among them is this soldier I found referenced in a battalion log entry:

16 Jan 69
0845H

require medevac for D co, line 114 [individual's numerical identification]. fine if left alone but whenever someone touches him, he begins foaming at the mouth.

With Tim due to leave country, battalion needed to promote another radio operator from one of its companies. Concerned it might be my old nemesis Gilmore, I asked Captain Blair for the guy's name.

"Don Nader?" I repeated back the name. There was a Don Nader who worked with me at Fort Huachuca. He also received orders for Nam and left a few days ahead of me. *Could it be him?* I wondered. The answer came a day or two later when Captain Blair escorted that very man into our tent and assigned him a cot. Don looked thinner than I remembered him in Arizona, and he was already rail thin there. He remembered me, of course, and Larry, too.

Back in our Huachuca days, Don and I always got along even though we ran in different circles. To me, he seemed more comfortable socializing with the West Coast, counterculture types than with my more conventional friends. I could better imagine him wearing a tie-dyed T-shirt and holding a peace sign than wearing Army fatigues and shouldering a rifle.

But all that changed in Nam. I thought he deserved great credit for persevering through all the hardships in the bush while humping a prick. When I got around to asking him about his time in the field, though, he flat out refused to discuss the topic. Thirty-eight years later, I located Don's phone number and called. Our conversation started out pleasantly enough. He told me he was a librarian in a large southern city, long married, and enjoying his grandchildren. I gave him my family history post-Vietnam, and asked if he could help fill in some gray areas for a book I was writing about the war. But just as he had done in Nam, he clammed up. Not ready to leave it at that, I asked him to at least help me with the names of those who served with us, if only for historical accuracy. The question seemed innocuous enough, and seeing that Don was a librarian, I thought "for historical accuracy" would play to his vocational instincts. He didn't bite; all I got was an abrupt "no." Since there was no point in pursuing the topic, I turned to lighter fare and asked about the weather in his neck of the woods. That's when he announced how it might be best if we end our conversation. Ouch. That was clear enough. Taking his lead, I wished him a good life and we hung up, never to speak again.

Don took an empty cot at the opposite end of the tent and stowed his gear. Later, I took him around the compound to meet some of the guys. At one point during his orientation, Don told me that he and fellow Fort Huachucan, Jay Walsh, arrived at battalion on the same day and that Jay went to Delta Company.

Jay Walsh. Now there's a name and face I would never forget. Jay was a short, pudgy-faced kid who always had a story for any topic of conversation. He also had this naive ability to roll with life's punches in blithe spirit. His unceasing cheerfulness, though usually refreshing, could also be annoying. But that was when I knew him stateside. A few weeks in the bush lugging a prick on his back would likely wipe any smile off his face.

Tim spent the few remaining days he had in country working closely with Don. During that time, radio traffic mounted due to an increase in enemy activity. As a possible prelude to a second Tet offensive, the communist North Vietnamese were pushing more men and materiel through our AO towards Saigon.

The North's easiest targets of opportunity were small stationary firebases around the Fishhook. They had names like Carolyn, Andy, Odessa, Jamie, Shirley, Aspen, Clara, Kelly, Ike, Becky, Rita, Mustang, Dot, and our firebase, Jake. First Cav Skytroopers and ARVN units defended most area bases, whereas Jake's chief defenders were the generally ill disciplined but very loyal Montagnards.

As a group, they easily panicked guarding the perimeter at night. Sometimes they followed procedure and sent up illumination flares to identify targets. All too often, though, one Yard would panic and fire his weapon under full automatic. That action would usually panic the Yard next to him into firing his weapon, which would cause the next Yard to panic. From there it was like falling dominoes. Before you could yell, "Cease fucking fire!" the entire perimeter would have erupted into unrestrained gunfire and exploding claymores—and all of it without first acquiring a target. Sometime later the firing would stop, hopefully because they listened to orders and not because they ran out of ammunition. With the perimeter finally quieted the rest of us could go back to sleep, secure in the knowledge the Yards were protecting us, if only with their bayonets.

On 9 December, Alpha Company was operating northwest of Quoin Loi near the edge of a rubber plantation when it bumped into a small group of North Vietnamese soldiers. After a pregnant pause, both groups opened up, and the gooks di di'd down rows of rubber trees.

Alpha Company took up hot pursuit, unaware that lying in wait among the rubber trees were two well-armed companies from the NVA 7th Division. And they were ready to fight. Early in the pursuit, the enemy opened fire, scattering the soldiers of Alpha Company behind rubber trees. Captain Talbott and company RTO, Davy Miller (my replacement in company), stayed together while Gilmore had somehow separated from them. Fourth Platoon pulled back to set up its mortar tubes.

Don and Tim were at the battalion radios when they heard Gilmore yell over the speakerphone, "Contact! Contact!" Word quickly got out that my old unit was under heavy fire. I rushed to the radios and found an assortment of officers and other personnel huddled around the communications table. Lieutenant Colonel McGraw had already left for his C & C helicopter to assess and assist from over the battle site.

The sounds of combat roared in the background whenever company radiomen keyed their handsets. My heart raced in empathy for the guys in my old unit, and I felt powerless to help until Tim relinquished his chair to me.

Bleed-over often garbled communications over the company radios. Gilmore, however, had no such problem. He operated the company's one and only battalion radio which was set to 5th Battalion's frequency. Amid the chaos, and despite not having Captain Talbott by his side, Gilmore constantly provided us with accurate, actionable information.

From his helicopter, Lieutenant Colonel McGraw conferred with Gilmore to coordinate cannon support. Gilmore came through like a champ, and for that Captain Talbott would later put him in for a Silver Star.

As the fighting continued, the opposition slid units behind Alpha's three rifle platoons and cut off the mortar platoon from the rest of the company. Caught in a deadly crossfire, 4th Platoon was getting torn up by the NVA. At the same time, the bulk of the enemy staged an all-out frontal assault on alpha's three rifle platoons. Enemy soldiers charged, zigzagging from tree to tree, exposing themselves within the gun sights of our Skytroopers. As one trooper told me after the battle, the gooks laughed wildly as they charged, as if they were on drugs.

The leader of 4th Platoon, a 2nd lieutenant, had been in country for only a few days. He frantically called for help, but for the moment Captain Talbott was powerless to assist. All three of his rifle platoons were currently pinned down. The men of the 4th would have to fend for themselves until the rest of the company extricated itself.

Fortunately for Alpha Company, a unit of armored personnel carriers (APCs) were in the area. Their eventual presence helped suppress the assault, which allowed Captain Talbott to maneuver back to 4th Platoon. When he gave the order to turn, the CP suddenly became the tip of the spear heading directly toward the besieged mortar platoon. The Old Man and his RTOs soon found themselves under withering fire. Davy ducked behind a rubber tree, as did the others for protection. Captain Talbott plopped down next to Davy and told him to find a tree. Davy looked at his captain and said, "I already got a tree!" They ended up sharing it.

The battle raged for five hours until the enemy broke contact at 1630H. Tragically, help came too late for the mortar platoon. Most of its men were killed or wounded, including the cherry platoon leader who died in the fight. Alpha Company killed a striking ninety-three enemy soldiers in battle, but it came at a heavy price. Fourteen of our troopers were KIA, seventeen WIA, and one MIA. The missing soldier was later listed as KIA when parts of his torso were found. He had taken a direct hit from a B-40 rocket.

The company's veteran First Sergeant, Earl Shaffer, had worked his way back to the 4th early in the fight. He exposed himself to enemy fire while caring for the wounded and died for his efforts. For his gallantry, our government bestowed upon him the Distinguished Service Cross (posthumously), our nation's second highest military decoration. Spider, the man who consoled me on that bunker at LZ Jack, took a round through the buttocks from friendly fire. He was still alive at battle's end. Doc worked feverishly to stop the bleeding, but he simply had lost too much blood. Spider knew he was going to die. He said so.

Alpha Company and the armor unit remained in the field overnight and sustained one mortar attack. The next day, what was left of Alpha Company flew to LZ Shirley before airlifting back to LZ Jake. Soon after they settled in, I crossed the bridge into camp and stepped inside the CP bunker. Captain Talbott and the XO were there, along with Gilmore and two or three others. Noticeably absent was Top Shaffer. The mood in the bunker was depressing, and only a few words were spoken.

I quietly sat with the men until I felt uncomfortably out of place. That's when I reiterated my sorrow for their losses and left. A few days later, I attended the memorial service and remembered the likes of Van Randolph, Mike Ray, and the young, green-eyed Tom Berkfield. After the service, I never bothered to revisit my old company.

After Tim left country, Lane, Digger, Larry, Don, and I remained to operate the battalion radios. By the end of December, Lane would be on his way home and Digger would have seniority, a position he would never abuse. We RTOs got along fine, at both work and play.

Larry's idea of play was to round up guys in the tent to bathe in the river down by the airstrip. Otherwise, men showered in a one-man plywood box located near the tent. It had a wooden pallet floor and walls high enough to cover one's privates, as if anyone cared. Suspended overhead was a large canvas water bag with a spigot at the bottom. Men generally waited to take their showers after the sun warmed the water.

One early morning I was sleeping on my cot when Larry shook me awake. He and five other guys were standing over me wearing only boxer shorts and boots. They were carrying green towels, soap, and their M-16s.

"Going to the river, let's go," Larry said flatly, as if he expected me to immediately jump off the cot. I looked at my watch and realized I'd been sleeping for maybe a couple of hours. I told him I just got off shift and for them to go without me.

"No, let's go. You can sleep later."

"Can't go this time, Larry. Too tired."

"No, let's go."

"Really, I'm not going."

"You're going."

"Dammit, Larry, leave me alone."

"Pussy."

"Asshole."

"Up yours."

Pleasantries out of the way, the gang of six exited the tent for the long downhill walk to the river, and I turned over and went back to sleep.

The next thing I remembered was waking up to an explosion outside the perimeter and hearing shouts of incoming. Men in our tent began running for the closest bunker, which was located at the back corner. I was right behind them shaking off mental cobwebs.

Enemy 82mm mortar rounds were exploding down at the airstrip. Their probable target was a C-130 transport that had recently landed to offload supplies. I could hear the plane's four turboprop engines powering up under full throttle to escape the barrage.

It was then I realized Larry and the others weren't in the bunker. *How long was I asleep,* I wondered. Digger and Nader were sitting nearby. They hadn't gone swimming. They also didn't remember seeing the bathers return. For now, all we could do was wait and hope for the best.

Located directly behind our tent were the battalion mortar pits. Men in the pits were busy returning fire with their 81mm and 4 deuce mortar tubes. Arty also joined in, returning fire from their 105mm cannons. When the attack ended several anxious minutes later, I jumped out of the bunker and raced to the top of a tall berm to get a view of the airstrip. The plane got off safely, but our bathing spot wasn't visible from my vantage point. I ran down the berm and headed for the TOC to alert the brass. On my way there, a jeep raced up from the direction of the airstrip and abruptly stopped in front of me. The lone occupant, an officer, suddenly slumped over the wheel. I could see him gasping for air and so I yelled for a medic. When Doc arrived, we helped the injured man to the closest cot, which happened to be in our tent. Doc ripped open the officer's shirt and discovered a small, bubbling hole in the man's chest. While he searched for a piece of plastic to cover the sucking chest wound, I ran to the TOC to arrange for a medevac. Lane was at the radios and put out the request. Then I turned to our operations officer to tell him about the bathers. He said he was aware of the situation and that someone was looking into it. A little while later, a call came in from the airstrip requesting a medevac. The news wasn't good. All six bathers, including Larry, were wounded in the mortar attack.

For the next several days our battalion chaplain received updates on the six men. Their lives were not in danger, we heard, although none was expected to return to duty. While I felt terrible for Larry and the others, I was also relieved to hear they would recover. Relieved, too, that I chose that particular morning not to bathe with them.

Several days later, our battalion chaplain came to us with some shocking news. One of the six bathers had died. It was Larry. I couldn't believe it; his wounds were supposedly non-fatal.

The way our chaplain had heard it from the doctors, Larry's physical injuries were not directly responsible for his death. He reportedly fell into a deep depression and lost his will to live. Bullshit, I thought. That wasn't Larry. Larry enjoyed life. Anyway, how could someone *will* himself to die, especially in a hospital setting with medical professionals there to intervene with medication and counseling? I kept telling myself there was more to the story. More than I would ever know.

Lieutenant Colonel McGraw was spending more time in his C & C helicopter flying from one contact to another. He liked hovering over his commanders in the field, like big brother watching out for his men. Sometimes he brought along an RTO, and always when he visited a company.

There were times during his flights when he'd lose radio contact with a distant field unit. In those circumstances, one of us at LZ Jake would relay his message. Our radios and tall mast antennas had to maintain constant communications with all companies in the field.

The following is an example of how I'd relay a message between the colonel riding in his C & C and a company commander in the field. Here, the colonel (Fast Flanker 6) tries to make radio contact with Bravo Company's commander (Leaping Scholar 6).

"Scholar 6, Flanker 6, over."

Scholar 6 doesn't answer because he cannot hear the call.

"Leaping scholar 6, Leaping Scholar 6, Fast Flanker 6, do you read, over?"

Still no answer.

At this point I might break in to assist. "Fast Flanker 6, Flanker 6-5, over."

"Flanker 6, over."

"Flanker 6, 6-5, do you wish me to relay, over?"

"Flanker 6, affirmative. Tell Scholar 6 to pat his head and rub his belly, over."

I have a pencil at the ready in case the colonel has a long message. Jotting down his key points spared me the certainty of catching hell were I to screw up his message.

"Flanker 6, 6-5, roger, break-break" (*break-break* informs battalion net I still have control). Without releasing the send button I initiate the relay.

"Leaping Scholar 6, Fast Flanker 6-5, over."

"Flanker 6-5, Scholar 6 India, over."

"Scholar 6 India, 6-5, I have a relay from Flanker 6 for your 6, over."

"Flanker 6-5, Scholar 6 India, wait one." Bravo Company's commander comes to the horn.

"Flanker 6-5, Scholar 6, over."

"Scholar 6, Flanker 6-5, I have a relay from Flanker 6, over.

"Flanker 6-5, Scholar 6, what is your message, over?"

"Scholar 6, 6-5, message as follows: Pat your head and rub your belly. End of message, over."

"Flanker 6-5, Scholar 6, don't you mean pat my belly and rub my head, over?"

"Scholar 6, 6-5, negative, over."

"Scholar 6, wilco (will comply), over."

"Scholar 6, 6-5, roger, break-break, Flanker 6, Flanker 6-5, over."

"Flanker 6, over."

"Flanker 6, 6-5, Scholar 6 says wilco, over."

"Flanker 6, roger, out."

"Fast Flanker 6-5, net clear."

On 15 December, battalion promoted me to the rank and pay grade of sergeant E5. I viewed the advancement as a great achievement, considering the fact that only two months earlier I was a specialist humping the bush with a twelve-man squad. The promotion had added significance in that it came with infantry stripes instead of specialist patches, which were more in keeping with my military specialty. Getting hard stripes meant 5th Battalion had accepted me into the ranks of the infantry, no small distinction. It would, I thought, qualify me to receive the coveted Combat Infantry Badge, an award given to infantrymen who fought in combat.

With the Christmas holiday fast approaching, care packages from home were on the increase. Troopers really enjoyed getting the gifts, especially those containing holiday cookies and the like. Gifts of liquor were also very popular, as were the men who received them. One evening, I shared the better part of a fifth of Jack Daniels with my newly discovered best friend who succumbed to my begging. After we drained the better part of it, I started out in the dark for the outhouse piss tube and ran my shin into a tent stake, gashing it. The numbing effects of alcohol tempered some of the pain, but as anyone knows, a hard blow to the shin always hurts like hell. Blood now running down my leg, I passed on the piss tube and hobbled over to the medical tent, where Doc recommended he stitch the cut. I recommended he not.

Against his better judgment, Doc applied butterfly bandages over the wound and wrapped it with gauze. I thanked him for not getting out his sewing kit and inquired in jest if he might consider putting me in for a second Purple Heart. He said if the Army had a medal for big babies, he would put me in for that. I ignored his attempt at humor (or mockery) and set out for the latrine. When I got back to my tent I downed several aspirin, not so much to relieve the leg pain as for my anticipated morning hangover.

The best present I got from home came from my brother Tom and his wife, Jan. When the package arrived, I eagerly opened it, thinking cookies or booze. Instead, I discovered something more valuable.

Popped popcorn!

This was the first time any of us had seen popcorn on base and it really caused a stir. That is, until a group of us discovered the corn to be stale and unsalted. While someone ran to find a saltshaker,

I kept wolfing down the almost good popcorn until I touched on a foreign object. It was a pint of some kind of sweet liqueur. Aha. Mystery solved—the popcorn wasn't there to eat, it was there to cushion the glass container. Salt now added to the box, several easy-to-please men helped me finish the popcorn and drain the bottle.

Afterward, I wrote Tom and Jan, thanking them for their two gifts. I said that while I didn't want to appear ungrateful, washing down stale popcorn with a sweet liqueur detracted a bit from the holiday charm. In response, they sent a larger care package. It contained a fifth of whiskey and several 1.5 ounce mini liquor bottles of assorted varieties—none sweet. They packed the bottles inside salted popcorn and sealed it all in plastic. Now the only things lacking were butter and a movie.

On the subject of movies, the special forces had a projector and some reel-to-reel movies, but they were loathe to loan them out or invite us in. To help relieve boredom in our tent, we participated in long bullshit sessions and played card games for hours on end. Hearts, oh hell, gin rummy, and poker were all popular. The only pot we had took the ante; it wasn't the smoking kind. If men got high on marijuana, they didn't do so openly. Or if they did, I was too drunk to remember. Anyway, when I was with Alpha Company in the field, I don't think troopers would have tolerated anyone getting stoned on missions in the bush.

During times of solitude, I wrote letters home and reread old missives while listening to American songs of the day broadcast over the Armed Forces Radio Network. One guy had a small reel-to-reel tape recorder and tapes dubbed with rock-and-roll songs. He'd occasionally let me borrow it at night. I'd lie on the cot, close my eyes, and dream of home with music playing quietly in my ear.

Toward the end of December, battalion brought in Jay Walsh to work the radios, and how he ever survived his months in the field, I could not imagine. But here he was now, a little less jovial and a lot less pudgy than I remembered him from Fort Huachuca. Unlike Don, Jay was willing to talk about his time in the field. He told me how his company commander let him hump within the CP *without* a radio for many weeks so he could get in shape and memorize company jargon. When Jay finally did strap on the prick, his transition, while not seamless, was less prone to failure, mistakes, and criticism. It was a good plan, one I now wished Captain Talbott had adopted with me. Maybe we could have spared everyone some grief.

Jay began his break-in period working days with another RTO while I rotated to the late shift. Working nights still didn't bother me. What *did* bother me was any number of annoyances that interrupted my sleep after my shift ended at 1000H. Topping my list of annoyances were the rising temperatures in the tent, and all the loud talking, particularly when troopers yelled "INCOMING!" Funny how one simple word could provoke me into running half-naked for the bunker.

During the month of December, enemy activity increased within our AO. Rifle companies were encountering more firefights in the field, and stationary firebases were taking more rocket and mortar attacks. LZ Jake certainly got its share:

18 Dec
incoming rounds LZ Jake 1 wia rec 8 rounds 107mm rocket 15-20 82mm mortar.

23 Dec
LZ Jake and CIDG Co. 3 US wia 2 US wia advisors 3 CIDG wia rec heavy volume of mortar and rocket fire throughout the day.

24 & 25 Dec
no mortar or rocket fire on Jake.

27 Dec
LZ Jake rec 30 82mm rounds.

28 Dec
LZ Jake rec 15-20 82mm mortar fire and engaged w/mortar.

29 Dec
5/7 LZ Jake 1 US kia 1 CIDG wia rec 74 rounds 82mm and rocket fire.

The 23 December attacks were numerous and particularly destructive. I was asleep on my cot when the first attack jolted me awake at 1100H. I leapt off my cot and along with everyone else, ran for cover. Mortar and rocket fire struck at the airstrip and the CIDG compound.

The second barrage occurred after lunch, at 1300H. By then I was dressed but dozing on my cot when the attack began. This time I stayed put and listened carefully to the explosions down at the airstrip. As long as the commotion was taking place downhill, I saw no reason to impulsively take flight. Shelling remained at the airstrip.

At 1600H, a third mortar and rocket attack hit the airstrip. This time, several men in the area didn't automatically run for bunkers. Instead, they took a wait-and-see attitude as I had done. Digger and I were listening to all the noise downhill when curiosity got the better of us. We thought it would be fun to climb a nearby berm to witness the action. From our lofty vantage point, we watched puffs of smoke and debris spray from exploding rounds on and near the airstrip. Several minutes later the attack ended, after our mortar pits and artillery offered return fire.

The fourth and final aerial barrage started at the airstrip at 1800H. And as we had done before, Digger and I climbed the berm to watch the action unfold. This time, the enemy had improved on its aim. One rocket scored a direct hit on our radar, knocking it out. Another struck our POL (petroleum, oil, and lubricants) dump adjacent to the airstrip. All the commotion lured several men to scale the berm to see for themselves.

Spectacular fireballs erupted from the storage site while the group of us stood on the berm marveling at the show. But then a curious thing happened. Those puffs of smoke coming from the mortars began puffing their way up our hill. Charlie was walking the rounds...*directly toward us!*

At that point, it was every dumbass for himself. I turned to hightail it and saw nothing but assholes and elbows racing down the berm. I sprinted for the aboveground TOC because it was close by, and I didn't like sitting in some rat hole bunker.

Rounds began raining down inside our perimeter. One scored a direct hit on the ammo dump adjacent to the TOC, setting it ablaze. The intense heat set off a chain reaction of crackling hellfire as stored ammunition began to "cook off." It sounded like a gun battle was taking place outside.

The RTO on duty placed two quick calls. One was a niner-niner apprising our companies of the situation in case we lost communications. The other call went out to HQ at brigade. Lieutenant Colonel McGraw expressed concern over the number of attacks the enemy had initiated in one day. He suspected the gooks might use this latest diversion to initiate an all-out ground attack. With that in mind, he ordered the camp on high alert. Everyone had to put on his helmet and flak jacket and have his rifle close at hand with extra magazines.

Captain Blair was standing next to me when the order went out. He turned my direction and mimicked the same "oh-oh" expression I had on my face. Neither of us had our gear, and neither of us wanted to run outside to collect it. I turned to redleg to see if he had his rifle and saw a "What the fuck now?" look on his face. Captain Blair thought a moment before coming up with a plan. He said only one of us need make the run. That seemed right. No sense putting three at risk when only one unlucky sap would do. But which sap?

I'm thinking rock, paper, scissors to break the deadlock when Captain Blair takes himself out of the running, proving once again that rank has its privileges. I turn to redleg. We're the same rank. He shrugs his shoulders, points to his radio, and mouths, "Can't leave my post." I feel like mouthing something back.

Effectively ending any discussion over who was going to make the run, Captain Blair taps me on the shoulder and begins issuing instructions. I'm thinking, *Okay, let's get this over with. How dangerous can cooking rounds be, anyway?* Not dangerous, according to Captain Blair. Cooking rounds don't actually shoot lead in the same way they would from a gun barrel, he says.

But when I peeked out the entrance and saw the dramatic light show ignite the evening sky, I came back to disagree. I told him bullets and shit were zinging all around outside and that only a crazy man would expose himself in the open.

"How about we wait for an actual ground attack before retrieving our gear?" I asked.

"Go ahead, but clear it with the Old Man first," Blair said, knowing I'd rather be dipped in a vat of acid than approach our commander at a time like this.

The captain tried again to assure me that the racket outside only *sounded* like bullets were zinging around. And he might have had me convinced until he handed me a borrowed flak jacket and helmet to wear. Reluctantly I put on the gear, returned to the doorway, and once again surveyed the scene. The exploding ammo dump was located far to my right. Dead ahead was my tent about twenty meters away. I recognized a few guys crouching behind the sandbags. *Maybe one of them owes me a favor. Forget it. There's no IOU big enough for this.*

The captain's tent was even farther to the left, but our TOC was between it and the cooking rounds. That would provide some protection on my run back, if in fact bullets were zinging in all directions as I had come to believe.

"Ahhh shhhit!" I bolted from the doorway running bent over with my eyes fixed straight ahead. My body felt heavy, like it was moving in slow motion. When I reached the entrance to the tent, I dove headfirst past the sandbags. A couple minutes later, I was back on the run lugging more equipment until I reached the captain's tent unhurt. The final leg of my journey was the least dangerous in my mind, albeit the most difficult. By now I was lugging three rifles, several ammunition belts, four helmets, and four flak jackets. I pretty much had to walk the rest of the way, but it hardly mattered. With all that body armor and gear, only a bazooka could have stopped me. When Captain Blair and redleg saw me appear at the door, they looked amused, I looked relieved, and the gooks looked to be nowhere in sight the rest of the night.

The following day was Christmas Eve, and if all went according to plan, both sides would stop shooting at each other. Our government had negotiated a twenty-four-hour ceasefire with North Vietnam so we could celebrate Christmas in peace. Known as the Christmas truce, it was set to begin at 1800H on the twenty-fourth of December. Our heavy weapons company at LZ Jake wanted to demonstrate their gratitude to the communists, so it sent them a "greeting card." At one minute before the truce was set to begin, all our big guns and mortars initiated a mad minute, firing every piece they had at a high rate of speed. *Merry Christmas, Charlie.*

Christmas Day, 1968, 2315H. Midnight was less than an hour away and I was sitting at the radios threading a three-inch reel of audiotape through a borrowed, handheld tape recorder. The truce had ended more than five hours earlier, and both sides had honored the ceasefire, at least in our AO. Fighting had yet to resume, and since the radios were unusually quiet, I thought this might be a good time to make a recording for the folks back home.

Earlier that same afternoon, a group of us celebrated the spirit of the day drinking spirits of the day. I mixed Federal Reserve whiskey that my brother Tom provided with eggnog Uncle Sam provided. At the entrance to our tent, someone perched a small Christmas tree atop the sandbags. It was artificial, of course, as was anyone's notion of "Peace on earth, good will toward men."

Overhead, a small airplane circled playing "Frosty the Snowman" and other yuletide carols over a loudspeaker. We sang along and ate cookies to help soak up the booze. Our intelligence officer, Captain Tenaka, came by with some kind of holiday candy he called preserved plum. He said he was in the giving mood, but I suspected he was trying to get rid of the stuff. It tasted nasty. A big grocery outlet in Chicago added some joy to the occasion by sending a large number of care packages to the troops. A few boxes even made their way to our distant outpost. From one box I grabbed the three-inch reel of blank audiotape that now lay threaded in the recorder.

The tape's recording time was limited to fifteen minutes per side, yet I had trouble filling it with meaningful thoughts. Sometimes I'd ramble. Occasionally I had to hit the pause button to avoid dead air. After rehearsing a few talking points, I pushed the record button for the first time: "Well hello, everyone, it's time for another fireside chat...."

The first thing I did was downplay the Purple Heart I had yet to receive. I did it to alleviate Moms growing anxiety as shown in her letters. On the tape, I told everyone that the cuts could have come as easily from scraping my hand against a tree. I also downplayed the rocket and mortar attacks at our airstrip without revealing the death and destruction they had caused inside our perimeter. I mentioned my upcoming R & R, set to begin 7 January. I told them how I looked forward to soaking in a bathtub and sleeping between white sheets on a real bed with a real pillow. "I took a lot of stuff for granted back home," I said on tape. "It's a lot different over here. Makes you appreciate all that's back home. All the friends and all the relatives, and especially the family. I'm really going to be happy to see you all again."

During my recording Lane walked in. He sat down on a metal chair next to me and began speaking in drunkenese. From what I could comprehend, he wanted to make a tape for his family. I reminded him that he was going home to Connecticut in five days and that he probably would arrive before the tape. All I got in return was a blank stare.

Before the tape came to an end, I wanted to demonstrate a companywide sitrep to the folks. At 2340H, I held the microphone up to the speaker and made the request. As expected, each man on watch whispered the words, "Sitrep green." Just as I wrapped up the call, the spool of tape ran down to a sliver. I finished the recording by saying that I hoped everyone at home had a great holiday.

This was one of three tapes I would send to my parents from LZ Jake. They kept two and I still have them today. In 2009 and 2010, the local radio station in Tomahawk, WI, transferred the tapes to digital CDs for me. WJJQ deejay Michael McGovern would not accept payment for his work or for the CDs, saying my service in war was payment enough. He has no idea how much those words meant to me.

The business of war resumed after the truce. Once again we received enemy rocket and mortar fire. Bunkers provided good protection from the attacks, but they were not one hundred percent mortar or rocket proof. A direct hit could collapse a bunker onto its occupants.

There is no more helpless feeling than sitting inside a bunker while bombs are exploding all around you. On one occasion, Nader and I were walking across base when a mortar attack began. We rushed for cover inside a small, aboveground hooch. The structure offered limited protection, which probably explained why we were alone. We squatted against one side of a sandbagged wall and listened to mortar rounds step closer to our hooch. *Swish-crack.* The ground shook from the concussion—either that or my knees were knocking. *Swish-CRACK.* Dirt sprayed the hooch. "That's way too close," shouted Don. He and I must have been thinking the same thing: the next round could drop directly on top of us. *Swish-CRACK.* Closer still, but this time the mortar leapfrogged over the hooch. We realized then we were out of immediate danger and breathed a sigh of relief.

On another daylight attack, a C-130 transport was taxiing near the airstrip when mortar rounds began exploding around it. Digger and I were again standing on the berm acting like a couple of cheerleaders, rooting for the plane as it revved its engines and raced down the runway amid a gauntlet of fire. The plane got off the ground, and as it careened safely away, we whooped it up for the lucky crewmen.

Not all aircraft escaped enemy fire at the airstrip. As an example, on 2 January 1969, rockets destroyed a C-130 while the plane sat idle overnight due to mechanical problems. The crewmen were safely billeted at the time—safe being a relative word.

"Gooks in the wire!"

Digger yelled his dire alarm from outside the TOC entrance one midafternoon. At about the same time, we heard small-arms fire coming from the special forces camp. The Green Beret RTO had called Digger, warning him that gooks breached the SF perimeter and were currently running through camp heading our direction. How they got through perimeter defenses in broad daylight wasn't important now, only that armed bad guys of unknown number were about to charge over our nearby earthen berm, the only barrier between the SF camp and us.

There were eight or so men in our tent when Digger put out the alarm. We all scrambled for our rifles, ammo belts, flak jackets, and steel pots. Everyone formed a defensive line behind the tent's three-foot-high sandbag wall and immediately opened boxes of fragmentation grenades. I sighted my rifle along the top of the berm and envisioned hoards of gooks charging over it at any moment. If we didn't stop them there, we'd have to fight them hand-to-hand.

Tension in the tent was off the charts. I needed to calm down.

"Don, grab a couple of beers and throw me one."

Not far from Nader sat a metal cooler loaded with iced beer for rationing that evening.

Don looked incredulous. "You're kidding, right?"

"Dead serious, man. Come on, get 'em."

Only when someone else yelled, "Yeah, get me one, too," did Don resign himself to the task. He duckwalked to the cooler, opened the lid, reached in, and began tossing cans of beer to the men, who passed around a church key. I poked holes in the lid and began gulping down the elixir, enjoying it every bit as much as a condemned man might enjoy his last cigarette. *They'll not get my beer, dammit.*

Shooting from the SF camp suddenly and inexplicably stopped. A couple of minutes went by when someone said, "What the hell's going on?" About then a really pissed off Digger burst into our tent. "Fuck it! Someone else can take over the fucking radios. I fucking quit!" *Yeah, Digger, like that's an option in Nam.*

Digger finally calmed down to a level somewhere above seething so he could tell us how the Green Beret RTO played him like a piano. When the call came in about gooks in the wire, Digger notified Lieutenant Colonel McGraw and then came out to warn everyone in the area. In the meantime, the colonel got on the horn with the special forces camp. The Green Beret RTO told him that they sighted gooks *near* the wire, not inside the wire, a claim Digger vigorously denied. The Old Man accepted the Green Beret version of events and had Digger's ass for lunch. But we knew better. Digger was too good a radioman to make that kind of mistake. He'd been had by the special forces, as I would be a few days later.

It happened while I was working a late shift. In the middle of the night I got a call from the Green Beret RTO. He sounded in great distress. His voice was barely audible from all his coughing and choking. "Say again, over?" I asked.

"Gas (cough)...attack (whoop)...drifting your direction (hack)."

Holy shit! I repeated back his words for verification, but there came no reply. *Double shit! The guy's passed out...or worse!*

Army basic training prepared me for gas attacks, but I never expected to face an actual threat from God knows what kind of chemical agent wafting our direction. The very thought of breathing in poisonous gas scared me more than hand-to-hand combat. There would be no time to lose. I jumped up and yelled, "GAS ATTACK, GAS ATTACK!" to warn the sleeping officers and then ran outside yelling the same alarm all the way to my tent. "GAS ATTACK, GET YOUR MASKS ON," I shouted to a somewhat unresponsive group while I fumbled with my own mask. Some of the guys thought I was yanking their chain and barely stirred. But most took me seriously and scrambled for protection. My warning duly given, I ran back to the TOC and found Lieutenant Colonel McGraw and Major Dalton sitting at my desk without their masks. The Old Man was casually speaking to the Green Beret RTO while I stood panting at the doorway looking foolish behind fogged up plastic lens covers. I was sorely tempted not to remove the mask to keep my identity unknown. Ultimately I did take it off, but I think the egg on my face maintained the disguise.

The Green Beret denied calling in a gas attack, but this time the Old Man wasn't taken in. At dawn he had a private conversation with the SF commander and that was the last of their practical jokes on 5th Battalion.

My scheduled separation date from Vietnam was also my last day of active service, and both were still months away. However, in the unlikely event the Army granted me an early out, I could expect to leave Vietnam and the active service three months early. In spite of near-impossible odds, brother Steve's correspondence helped keep my hopes alive. There was, he said, an angle he was still working on.

It occurred to me that if I got an early out, I might miss the opportunity to go on R & R (rest and recreation). So in early December, I put in for R & R to Taipei, Taiwan over other available destinations. The list of countries and cities sounded so exotic to me, places like Bangkok, Hong Kong, Hawaii, Australia, Manila, Penang, Tokyo, Kuala Lumpur, and Singapore. Vung Tau and China Beach were in-country options, but I never considered vacationing in war-torn Vietnam.

Tipping the scales in favor of Taipei came from a photo I saw in a magazine. The picture showed a scantily dressed Asian beauty giving a massage to a contented-looking GI. The accompanying article suggested that any soldier looking for hassle-free female companionship would do well to choose Taipei. Bingo! When does my plane leave? I wasn't looking for a soul mate, nor was I interested in the dating game. No, with only five full days to unwind in another country, I had certain priorities requiring expediency of purpose.

Before the New Year, that much-anticipated envelope from brother Steve arrived. I eagerly ripped into it, hoping the contents would prove to be the equivalent of a plane ticket back home. Instead, my enthusiasm turned to disappointment.

Two documents were in the envelope, and taken together, I suspected their combined weight would do little to advance my cause. The first document was a letter of acceptance back into SIU for spring quarter classes. Good to that point. But the letter also stipulated my status to be "conditional," which is to say, probation. I knew the Army would take a dim view of anything less than good standing.

The second document, the bold one I needed to close the deal, was weak. It came from the history department where Steve had completed his graduate work. He sought support from the department's acting dean who proved sympathetic to my cause, which was hardly a surprise considering the anti-war mood on college campuses across America at that time. She agreed to write a letter on my behalf, and so under the department's letterhead, she expressed interest in my joining the department to resume a degree in history.

What? A degree in history? That was news to me. The only history courses I took in college were a couple of freshman level classes that I probably didn't attend anyway. Fortunately, my transcripts were not included. Even so, I was sure to face the monumental task of convincing high-ranking military officers, themselves college graduates, to take these documents, and me, seriously. Dispirited, I folded the papers and put them away.

Sometime during the first week of January, my orders for R & R came through. I was granted five days in Taipei from 12 to 17 January, and with a generous five days off on either side, possibly allowing for my remote outpost. With all that spare time, I decided to visit my old Fort Huachuca buddy, Eldon Smith. The lucky stiff was stationed at a personnel office in Bien Hoa. Without delay, I dashed off a letter saying he shouldn't be surprised if I showed up.

Maybe a day or two before leaving for R & R, I mustered the courage to approach Captain Blair and ask his permission for an early out. Without even asking to see my documents, he said he wouldn't stand in the way. *Could it really be this easy?* I wondered. So on my first day of R & R, I took a chopper to Quan Loi where I asked a battalion clerk to grind out the necessary paperwork. He took down all my information and promised to have everything typed upon my return. *Super. Another hurdle jumped.*

I remained at Quan Loi overnight and flew to Bien Hoa the following morning. Once there I found my friend, Eldon, waiting for me. After he helped me secure a bunk with a real mattress, we toured the grounds and caught up on the past few months. I tried to keep the conversation upbeat to avoid spoiling the mood. At one point, Eldon said he had attended the Bob Hope USO Christmas show recently held at base. Not to be outdone, I told him Victor Charles put on several good shows at LZ Jake. In fact, they were a *blast.*

Somewhere in the conversation I asked Eldon how much free time he could devote to my visit. He said he had nothing but free time, and explained why. Before leaving for Nam, Eldon made his own plans for an early out to further his education. He brought with him his college transcripts from Arizona State showing he earned a B.A. and a letter of acceptance into graduate school at Southern Illinois University. Eldon liked college, and it wasn't by coincidence that he chose SIU to continue his studies. I had encouraged him to do so at Fort Huachuca. All this I knew. What I didn't know was that the Army had granted his request. Moreover, his section chief had already replaced him. So here was my fortunate friend left with no clearly defined responsibilities...more than two months ahead of his DEROS.

Somehow I got over my feelings of jealously and joined Eldon in his new hobby of photography. For the better part of two days, we drifted around the large base taking rolls of pictures using his cameras. Then we developed our black and white film in a darkroom, and made prints of various sizes. Many of my pictures came out over or underexposed, or grainy. But others turned out quite good. I even rolled a few inside a shipping tube and mailed them home.

On my fourth travel day, I flew up to An Khe to retrieve my khakis. Several soldiers were on the flight, including an all-too-familiar face: my ex-platoon sergeant, Staff Sergeant Carter. Whatever the reason for his being here, this helicopter wasn't big enough for the two of us. I kept my distance from my second least favorite GI but made sure he could see the three stripes on my sleeves. After the helicopter landed and everyone debarked, Sergeant Carter approached me with a grin on his face. Whatever nonsense he was up to, he would quickly learn I was not the same man he could intimidate a few months earlier. Regardless of his extra stripe, if the guy gave me any crap, he was going to hear all the things I had only dreamt of telling him while in Alpha Company.

What he *did* say caught me completely off guard. Without a hint of sarcasm, he congratulated me on my promotion. While I enjoyed hearing his compliment, I was still wary of his sincerity. So rather than hang around and risk more disappointment, I politely thanked him and excused myself, saying I had errands to run.

My first stop was at the paymaster's office where I collected about four hundred dollars. From there I walked to the post exchange to buy a small Kodak camera and a new wristwatch. The shutter on my old camera had rusted in the bush, and the Timex winding pin had worn smooth to where I could no longer grasp it. I eliminated the winding problem by buying a self-winding Seiko watch. It cost twenty-eight dollars, came with a fancy day/month display, and included a comfortable Twist-O-Flex wristband.

From the PX, I walked to the mess hall and shuffled through the lunch line filling a metal tray with hot food. When I turned to find a seat, there was Sergeant Carter waving me over to his empty table. Cursing under my breath, I reluctantly joined him.

To my relief, our conversation over chow went surprisingly well; only one time did he veer into choppy waters when the topic of my "good-natured" ribbing came up. He said he would have cut me slack in his platoon had he known I was an infantryman instead of a non-infantry radio operator. When I told him I *was* an O5B radio operator, he looked again at my sleeves and asked how come the hard stripes and not specialist patches? It was my turn to grin. "Cause I'm good," I said.

In the middle of our lunch, base sirens sounded the alarm. Soldiers bolted for the exit doors faster than if someone had cut a beer fart in a pup tent. Within seconds, the building was pretty much empty with the exception of Sergeant Carter, me, and maybe a half dozen other men who remained eating. We didn't join the jackrabbits to the bunkers and instead listened for a reason to abandon our warm meal. From a distant part of the compound we barely heard a few muffled explosions, so we stayed put. Several minutes later, the all clear sounded and soldiers began funneling back through the doors to take up their cold lunches. Sergeant Carter and I smiled at each other as we got up to scrape off our trays. Outside we shook hands, and with our newfound mutual respect, we went our separate ways.

On my fifth and final day of in-country travel, I flew to Cam Ranh Bay and spent the night. The next day—my first official day of R & R—I had to wait until 1800H to board a flight for Taipei, arriving there after dark. During the military bus ride from the airport to the R & R center, a sergeant instructed us on the do's and don'ts while in the Republic of China. Basically, he said, don't kill anybody, don't give a prostitute all your money, and wear a condom if you mud the turtle.

After signing in at the center, we loaded onto civilian buses for a complimentary ride downtown. Our first stop was in an area of the city that featured bars offering female companionship, for a price. Anyone not interested could remain on the bus for a trip to the hotels. By the time our bus arrived at the first stop, every man was out of his seat pushing toward the door. Of course I had no desire for beer and babes. But when the bus door opened, a crush of horny, thirsty men pushed me off the transport against my will. Before I could claw my way back on board, the bus door shut and the driver sped away. Cold and alone, and with nowhere else to go, I entered the nearest bar...and gleefully pulled out my wallet.

Cutting to the chase, her professional name was Snow (not to be confused with "as white as the driven"). And of those three cautionary statements from our guide on the bus, I followed the first one and didn't kill anybody. I did, however, give Snow most of my American dollars to cover our expenses for the five days, including hotel, meals, tips, a circus performance, a long taxi ride to a mountain temple, and, well, her companionship.

I also made sure to keep enough money to pay for a massage at a nearby parlor. It was there that a scantily dressed masseuse prepared me for my inaugural massage. She first had me strip and sit inside one of those old-fashioned steam boxes, the kind with a hole at the top for your head to poke through. Then she wrapped a towel around my neck to keep in the steam and cranked up the heat to somewhere between parboil and poach. Afterward, she gave me a cold beer of divine proportion to drink under a cool shower. Then the diminutive masseuse had me lie on a table for what began as a sublime rubdown. She had a real talent for kneading and poking me. A light dusting of flour and you could have confused me with the Pillsbury Doughboy. I was loving it all, right up until the sweet thing transformed into a scary dominatrix. She jumped on the massage table and began walking up and down my back and buttocks with her bare feet. I gritted my teeth hoping she wouldn't collapse a lung or crush a kidney. Thankfully, she dropped to the floor before inflicting permanent damage; however, the sadist hadn't finished with me. She picked up two small blocks of wood and proceeded to pound my already abused muscles into pulp. Not wanting to sound wimpy, I let her have her way until the torture got so bad that I would have gladly traded it for a Vietnam firefight. Just as I was about to accuse her of being a communist sympathizer, she changed tactics. Putting down the blocks, she had me roll over and found a way to put a smile on my face.

Snow and I spent two nights in an austere hotel room somewhere in the city. On the second day she offered up her small apartment for us to stay in. I went along with the idea, even when the hotel manager refused to refund any unused portion of the money Snow paid up front. My guess is the manager and she split the kitty. Before we checked out, I summoned a tailor, who fitted me with two twenty-five dollar suits, one of which included a lapel-less Nehru jacket. In addition to the suits, I bought a sweater to ward off the outside chill at night.

Snow either failed to communicate or could not communicate in English that *her* apartment was actually her *parent's* apartment. I felt uneasy with the arrangement, but Snow's parents treated me with utmost kindness for what little I saw of them. They stayed elsewhere most of the time, possibly with relatives, to give us privacy. Snow likely compensated them for their inconvenience with the money she was to use on my behalf.

On the fifth day at 0345H (yes, the ungodly hour of 3:45 A.M.!), Snow waited with me outside the R & R center for a bus to take military personnel back to the airport. While we waited in the dark for the bus to arrive, she cried crocodile tears and held me tight while I made sure she wasn't lifting my wallet. We hardly spoke, but then we didn't speak a whole lot anyway. She knew only a few words of English, and most of those were related to her profession, including her favorite string of words, "Me need mo mony." Although her business interests and my carnal interests had come to an end, I had little doubt that in five days hence she would be standing at the same R & R center shedding those same crocodile tears for her next GI. For her, saying goodbye would come easy. My goodbye was harder in that I was leaving a peaceful country for another suffering the pangs of war. Still, anything I felt would surely pale in comparison to our married soldiers, many of whom chose Hawaii or Australia to spend R & R with their spouses. Leaving their loved ones behind would have been the hardest of all goodbyes.

With five more days travel time ahead of me, I took a couple of side trips, beginning with Bien Hoa to spend more time with Eldon. Two days later, I landed at Saigon's Ton Son Nhut airbase intending to tour the capital city and spend the night. Much to my surprise, officials wouldn't allow me to enter Saigon, stating it was temporarily off limits to 1st Cavalry field units. Apparently, Cav soldiers had caused too much trouble with the civilian population and military police. So instead of roaming Saigon for the day, I had to cool my jets at a military facility called Camp Alpha.

The next day I flew back to An Khe to stow my khakis and spend the night. Late that following afternoon, I was back at Quan Loi and inside the battalion clerk's office to pick up my typed paperwork. A clerk looked around and found my original documents still untouched in the same basket. For two weeks the papers had sat there collecting red dust. I was upset at the clerks for letting the work slide, and mad at myself for not anticipating an Army SNAFU.

Had I not taken those side trips and instead come directly to Quan Loi, I could have maintained pressure on the clerks to type the papers. As it was, all I could do was accept another one of their promises and leave camp having precious little time remaining to process out of Vietnam.

Disappointed but well rested, I returned to LZ Jake in time to work an overnight relay on the top of a distant mountain. Captain Blair collected his RTOs and asked for a volunteer to accept the assignment. Initially, his appeal fell on deaf ears, as it was our custom never to volunteer. But when no one else stepped forward, I felt pressure to accept the assignment. You see, ever since that night when I raced from tent to tent dodging cooking rounds, my relationship with Captain Blair had strengthened. He thought I was a brave guy who was good on radio, and he was right, but only half-right; my radio skills were good. The brave part was myth, except I didn't have the heart to dispel it. So when our section chief asked for a volunteer and no one stepped forward, the only way to perpetuate the myth was to take the assignment. *What the hell*, I thought, *how big a deal could it be anyway?*

Afterwards the guys thanked me for my lapse of good judgment. They also wanted to know if I wasn't doing a bit of brown-nosing. Their jab was mostly good-hearted, but it needed addressing before their suspicions gained traction. I reminded them that a brown-noser typically curried favor and how that didn't apply to me since I was the one flying off to some bumfuck so they could lallygag about the tent pulling their puds. Talk about a lack of gratitude. Couldn't they see I was doing them a favor?

Although the particulars of the assignment are lost in memory, I think some units of 5th Battalion airlifted into the vicinity of the Black Virgin Mountain located a few kilometers northeast of Tay Ninh City. At the time, there was a lot of fighting in the area. My job was to relay messages from the mountaintop between our units below and LZ Jake, Quan Loi, Phouc Vinh, or a combination of those. The mountain itself covered ten square kilometers and ascended something like 1,000 meters off the jungle floor. South Vietnamese forces owned the top of the mountain. Everything below was Indian country.

On the afternoon of my assignment, a Huey slick dropped me onto a small ARVN compound on the peak. A South Vietnamese soldier was waiting there to lead me inside a communications bunker where only ARVNs were sitting at the radios. I don't remember seeing another American, which was hardly reassuring. In fact, it made me feel downright anxious knowing that my safety might depend on ARVN soldiers who were reputedly unreliable in battle, and battles were in progress below us.

The sights and sounds of war continued throughout the night. Aerial flares regularly lit up the black sky. AC-47 Spooky aircraft circled the mountain rattling off their mini-guns, sending streams of red tracers snaking toward the ground. The staccato sounds of small-arms fire punctuated the air down the mountain. Artillery cannon pounded the jungle.

I relayed messages all night on the radios without benefit of sleep, although the constant cacophony outside would have prevented that, anyway. By morning my nerves were shot. The good news was the heaviest fighting had ended, as had my assignment. I dragged myself aboard another slick bound for LZ Jake, vowing once again never to volunteer.

The threat of another massive January Tet offensive passed without the same number of coordinated attacks as the year before. The '69 Tet was still deadly, but our military forces were better prepared this go-around. Cav Division played a key role in disrupting the enemy's push toward Saigon. And yet the war continued, as it would for several more years, even as we kept winning the battles.

One night at LZ Jake, a large, hungry rat crawled into Nader's cot and used him as a buffet. Don's rude awakening brought screams from him and the rat (it was hard to tell who had the highest pitch). Screams in the night were usually due to nightmares or rat bites. Nader would have both. His nightmare began that next morning with a series of painful rabies shots administered around his belly button. Those shots would continue over the next several days.

While on the subject of two to a cot, a young Asian prostitute and her old, wrinkled pimp appeared in camp one early evening and set up shop in a small hooch. All officers and high-ranking NCOs were oddly AWOL, which made me suspect they were aware of the situation but kept a blind eye. Word spread quickly among the troops, and before long a line formed at the front of the hooch. As GI after GI entered the temporary brothel, Digger and I watched the procession from a distance while sitting on sandbags outside our tent drinking beer. We were no prudes, but pulling train wasn't our idea of fun. There were many others who felt as we did, but even so, the line maintained itself into the evening. By the time the caboose left the train yard, Digger and I were half drunk and fully curious to have a look inside (yes, only a look), and so we walked over to the screen door and stole a peek. There on the cot was the young prostitute, leaning in a fetal position up against the old papa-san. She was partially covered in cloth; her eyes were closed; her skin ashen. The pimp was stroking her tangled, sweaty hair when he caught sight of us. Thinking we were new customers, he scolded us away in Vietnamese. Put off by the sight, we gave him the finger and returned to our tent. The next morning our guests were gone.

Digger's tour of duty was winding down and battalion would soon need a replacement. I had more than a passing interest in the matter and asked Captain Blair about his list of candidates. He said the decision had been made and that Alpha Company was sending up the new man.

Oh, no, say it ain't so.

It was so. Gilmore was our new RTO.

Captain Blair saw the sour expression on my face and asked if something was wrong. I told him that Gilmore and I had a personality conflict when we served together in company and how it might affect my job at battalion. He tried to reassure me by saying Gilmore would find himself back in the field if he didn't respect my rank and position, the position of senior RTO. And as a way to emphasize my new status to Gilmore, he gave me a new call sign: Fast Flanker 6-5 *mike*.

"Fast Flanker 6-5 mike." The words seemed to lilt over the tongue with ego-inflating timbre. "Fast Flanker 6-5 *mike*." I said again, putting emphasis on the word *mike*. I couldn't wait to adopt the new call sign. Unfortunately, any enthusiasm I felt was lost on my fellow RTOs. When they heard the news (doubtless from me), I got beaucoup shit for trying to be a big shot. To keep peace in the family, I fought the urge to use the fancy new call sign and would have completely succeeded if it were not for Gilmore. After he arrived at battalion and occasionally sat with me at the radios, I couldn't help but sneak in the word mike to remind him of my climb to the mountaintop. It was a juvenile stunt but oh so gratifying.

Sometime in early February, battalion had my paperwork typed and ready for pickup. Leaving nothing to chance after all the delays, I flew to Quan Loi and collected the documents myself. While there, I asked to present them directly to battalion's personnel officer for review. For whatever reason, my request was denied. Without the opportunity to state my case and answer the inevitable questions my submission would elicit, I had to leave the documents for review and hope for the best.

Toward the latter part of February, communist North Vietnamese initiated a weak offensive on major southern cities, including Bien Hoa and Long Binh. Their attacks were not as coordinated or widespread as those of the '68 Tet. After the offensive, 3rd Brigade ordered our 5th Battalion to prepare for redeployment for parts yet unknown, but still within III Corps.

By 26 February, 5th battalion had established its forward operations on LZ Buttons, located about 30 kilometers northwest of Quan Loi. Also by that date, I had yet to hear anything from battalion personnel. My frustration only grew with each passing day until I began to think someone was playing a cruel joke, intentionally stalling a decision so as to foil my plans. But then the day came when the envelope holding the decision arrived. I eagerly opened it and scanned the cover letter, looking for the words "granted" or "approved." What I saw instead was "request denied."

I shook my head. It wasn't supposed to turn out this way, not after my brother's dedicated work, my parents' expectations, and my recent efforts. But there it was, request denied. Reluctantly, I took the news to Captain Blair, who detected my disappointment.

"Maybe you can appeal," he suggested, trying to sound supportive.

I appreciated the thought, but the idea left me cold. Because of all the delays, I told him there probably wasn't enough time to submit an appeal. Besides, who in authority would be inclined to hear it anyway. And there was another reason steering me away, one which I kept to myself. It was that I couldn't face another emotional roller-coaster ride, having my hopes rise only to have them dashed again from rejection. Captain Blair said he would be pleased to keep me around for the next three months, but suggested again that I consider an appeal to our battalion XO about getting the decision overturned.

Major Schiano. Although I didn't know our executive officer very well, I did see him as approachable and fair-minded. These were all necessary traits if he were to consider helping me. The major spent most days at Quan Loi, but after our move to LZ Buttons, he was spending more time at our LZ helping Lieutenant Colonel McGraw. And he was in camp now.

Before I decided what to do, I returned to my tent to pour over Steve's handiwork and the Army's letter of rejection. I was looking for anything that would help me avoid another train wreck. Nothing good came of it; it still looked like a train wreck. Badly as I wanted to make an appeal, I felt sure that any additional effort on my part would only lead to more failure and embarrassment. I decided to accept my fate and serve the next three months in Vietnam. Reluctantly, I resealed the documents and buried them under my cot.

They didn't stay buried for long.

Credit Gilmore. All he had to do was walk inside the tent to provide me with all the motivation I needed to take up the appeal.

While Gilmore's switch to battalion RTO began smoothly enough (he was careful with everyone), before long he fell back into his old ways, acting self-important to men of equal or lower rank and kissing up to the brass. Nothing terribly overt, just cleverly subtle. And it was so unnecessary. Gilmore was a damn good radio operator in spite of his proclivity to crawl under my skin. He was sharp as a tack, and he exhibited reasonable calm and efficiency on radio during stressful situations. Those traits alone would have put him in good stead with the brass.

Convinced I would go dinky dau alongside him in the coming months, I grabbed the envelope from under the cot and set out to find our battalion executive officer. I hoped he possessed great compassion...and an even greater sense of humor.

"You got balls, Hoffmann," said Major Schiano after looking over the documents.

"Yes, sir, but will you help me?"

The major could have easily avoided the matter. Even if he were inclined to get involved, I currently had less than three weeks to process out of Vietnam *and* separate from the Army—a seemingly impossible timeline given my remote location and the Army's sluggish bureaucracy. That's why his offer to help stunned me.

As the battalion's executive officer, he authorized my early out request at battalion level, but cautioned me that the next level up, brigade, would also have to give *its* stamp of approval. He expedited the paperwork, and then to save time, had me carry it to brigade's personnel office back at Quan Loi. Over a week passed before the decision came down. Brigade rescinded the authorization.

My early-out deadline was now only a week away, and so it was understandable Major Schiano was ready to throw in the towel, saying I had fought the good fight. But I wasn't quite ready to get out of the ring and gently pressed the major to come up with any other idea, no matter how fantastic. He paused to think a moment. The only option left to me, he said, was an appeal to division, and the mere idea of it made him chuckle. For one thing, we had almost certainly run of time. For another, division would very likely side with brigade, assuming someone would even hear my appeal at division.

"But there's still a chance, no matter how slim, is that right, sir?"

In the longest of long shots, he authorized me to fly up to division rear at An Khe and see if someone inside the offices of the chief of staff—the supreme court over personnel—would hear my appeal. Anything to get me off his back, I thought.

The day after our talk, I was standing inside the air-conditioned building for the chief of staff at An Khe, introducing myself to a clean-shaven Spec 5 seated behind the front desk. The indifferent REMF was smartly dressed in a new uniform and with nary a hair out of place. In stark contrast to him stood this bewhiskered GI smelling of sweaty eau d'latrine, wearing clean but worn fatigues, scuffed boots, and a weather-beaten ruck. My M-16 was in one hand and my mud-stained helmet was tucked under an arm.

The clerk-and-jerk looked properly unimpressed. "What can I do for you, sergeant?"

To help warm up the dour fellow, I smiled and commented on how good the air-conditioning felt. His face remained unchanged and the room suddenly got chillier. Taking his cue, I scrapped the small talk and presented my paperwork. I also asked to speak to someone with authority who might act on my behalf. Without bothering to look at the documents, he asked. "Do you have an appointment?" I told him no but that my battalion XO had me fly in from my small firebase in III Corps to speak to the chief of staff.

Finally a smile came to his face. "That's impossible," he said. "You can't speak to the colonel without an appointment." He went on to say that all requests of my nature were handled through established paperwork channels and not face-to-face interviews. Trying not to sound argumentative, I explained how my circumstances were unique in that I didn't have time go through all the proper channels. Therefore, I needed approval ASAP.

The clerk wanted to know why I waited so long to make the submission. I stretched the truth by telling him the situation was beyond my control because the university had only recently sent the documents. "As you can see, specialist, I had no choice but wait."

When he hesitated, I saw my opening.

"Will you help me out, specialist? I know this is unorthodox, but I went through a lot and came a long way to be turned down now."

Without a word he got up holding my paperwork and walked down the hall into another room. Moments later, he returned empty-handed and had me take a seat. Minutes passed when his phone buzzed. "Lieutenant Brock will see you...down the hall, first door on the left."

The officer saw me at the open door and waved me in. I walked to the front of his desk and reported at attention. From the corner of my eye I could see him eye me from head to foot. "Just get out of the field, sergeant?" he asked, looking mildly amused.

I apologized for my attire and related the circumstances behind the urgency to reach these headquarters from my small firebase in III Corps. He had me take a seat and went right to the documents. Before long, a frown came to his face.

"This is all you have?"

I anticipated this question and decided to try a new tactic, known as the power of positive bullshit. I told the lieutenant there was a bigger picture to consider, that of a young man who had once led an aimless, undisciplined life until the Army turned him around. I explained how my Vietnam experience had given me the discipline and maturity to finish my college studies and earn a doctorate in history.

Apparently, the lieutenant couldn't picture my bigger picture, sympathetic though he was. He denied my request for an early separation, saying that were he to grant it, his superior officer, Captain Dettmer, would overrule it anyway. Hearing that, I asked if I could put in a personal appeal with the captain. He said no and assured me that any effort on my part would only be a waste of everyone's time.

The lieutenant was about to dismiss me when I quickly changed the subject and began talking off topic, hoping to improve our rapport. The ploy worked. After a few minutes of small talk, I returned to our original topic and gently encouraged him to allow my appeal. This time he gave in. He left the room to speak with the captain. When he came back, I was handed my paperwork and told to go down the hall and report to Captain Dettmer. I couldn't believe my incredible good luck. *Maybe I can pull this off after all.*

"Sir, Sergeant Hoffmann reporting as ordered, sir."

A stern-looking Captain Dettmer returned my salute but held me at attention, usually not a good sign. The officer walked from behind his desk, put his face next to my ear, and proceeded to berate me for appealing Lieutenant Brock's decision. At some point I was able to interject an apology and attempted to explain how I might not have properly clarified my position to the lieutenant. The captain cut me off. Not only was he not interested in hearing my appeal, he ordered me back to my battalion on the next available flight and then summarily dismissed me. Under any other circumstance, I would have immediately performed an about-face after been given a direct order. But this wasn't any other circumstance.

"Sir, can I appeal your decision?"

"What?! No!" he shouted in my ear. "The decision is mine and it is final. You are dismissed, sergeant!"

Nothing ambiguous there. About face. Out the door. Fini.

It's late afternoon now, and the first flight back to Quan Loi isn't until the next day. Fine. I would get lost in my cups at the NCO club on base. But first I had to call 5th Battalion HQ.

Jay Walsh took the call and summoned Major Schiano, who got on the horn. He listened quietly as I detailed my day, putting emphasis on the captain's refusal to both read my documents and allow an appeal. When I finished, the major told me to call him back in the morning before my flight, but he wouldn't explain why.

The following morning I did as instructed and received some incredible news. Major Schiano had somehow arranged a brief appointment for me to see the colonel himself. He couldn't hide his surprise, and I couldn't hide my utter appreciation. I left the communications center filled with excitement knowing I would get one final hearing. [Some forty years later I was able to contact retired "Colonel" Schiano. He was very nice on the phone but said too many years had passed for him to remember the event].

As the morning wore on, my excitement turned into anxiety. I thought, How can I ever hope to gain favor with a bird colonel knowing what he's going to read? I'll be lucky if all he does is throw me out of his office.

I still had plenty of time before my appointment to shower, shave, and rub boot black on my scuffed boots. I also worked on my oral presentation, which needed life support. Up to now, I had relied on a wing and a prayer to gain an early release, but neither of those had worked, probably because facts and reason stood in the way. I needed something else—something that would transcend logic.

Emotion. That's it! Pour on the emotion.

Who was I kidding? This was a bird colonel here—stoic, serious-minded figures all. But what other choice did I have? Exactly none. So I wracked my brain for an emotional hook, one so heartfelt that it would bring tears to a dead man...maybe even a living colonel. With my luck, though, his tears would come from laughter.

At the appointed time, I'm once again in the building for the chief of staff, standing in front of the specialist's desk. Funny, he's showing a little more respect. He asks me to take a seat and I do so within the confines of the air-conditioned waiting room. Minutes drag before he has me proceed down the hall to the last door on the right, past the offices of the lieutenant and captain.

On my way, I look into the lieutenant's room. He pretends not to see me. Moving along, I glance into the captain's room. He's staring at me with threatening eyes. *Rat bastard.* He probably told the colonel I disobeyed his direct order and I'm here to be brought up on charges. Long Binh jail, here I come.

The colonel summons me through his open door. He's sitting behind a large, uncluttered desk. There is at least one window to the outside. It's shut but not shaded. I stand at attention and report with a crisp salute. He responds with a three-quarter salute and has me take a seat.

The colonel studies my documents while I wait for the hammer to drop. He looks up. He looks down. He looks up and asks about my unit. He wants to know where it's located, and how much fighting we're experiencing. I'm not expecting small talk and must switch mental gears to form my answers. He then asks about my military background. I tell him. Now comes the sticky part of the conversation. The colonel wants to know why I deserve an early out to continue my education when my record clearly shows a lack of commitment to higher learning. I anticipated this question and divulge the reason for my poor grades. Actually, "the" reason was not the only reason. But the other reasons, like skipping the study room for the barroom, or attending purple passion parties (house parties that featured grain alcohol and grape juice mixed in bathtubs), would have done little to advance my cause.

In some detail, I tell the colonel that my downward spiral began after my high school sweetheart surprised me with a "Dear John" letter in the middle of my freshman year. I tell him we dated all four years in high school and that we were in a serious relationship. Learning of our breakup crushed me, and that caused me to lose focus on my academics.

My story, while based in fact, was an exaggeration. It's true her letter contributed to my lack of focus, but my life was destined to take the same path, anyway. I was simply too young and irresponsible at that time to be confined to the disciplines of college or consigned to a marriage.

Colonel Bowen pensively listens until I finish. "But you're ready to commit yourself to school now?"

"Yes, sir, the Army put my life back into perspective, sir. I look forward to continuing my studies, sir."

"You've put a lot of effort into this, haven't you?"

"Yes, sir, along with the help of many others, including Major Schiano and my section chief, Captain Blair, sir."

"And you've been persistently annoying, my staff tells me."

"I'm sorry if that's been the case, sir. I just want to go back to college."

The colonel stares at me a few moments longer and then looks down at his desk. Almost imperceptibly he shakes his head side to side.

Being judge, jury, and executioner, I do hereby find the defendant....

Colonel Bowen raises a hand and slams it down on the desk. I jump in my seat. *My God, I'm dead.*

He looks up at me, "Against my better judgment, sergeant, I'm granting your request."

The room spins. I'm stunned. Too stunned to speak.

"Now, when again is your date of early separation?"

I fumble for the date before coming up with it.

He looks at his calendar. "Christ, you might not have enough days to process out of the Army before that date.

No, no. Don't change your mind. "Sir, whatever it takes, sir, I'll do it."

The colonel looks at his watch. He tells me to return in a few hours to pick up my expedited orders. He'll get me stateside, he says, but if folks there don't have time to process me out of the Army, I'll have to serve out my final three months of active service somewhere back in the States. With that he is up and out the door before I can stand and salute.

I remain seated in his office to calm myself. Everything around me feels surreal, like I'm in a dream. When I finally do get up, I look outside the window and see the colonel walk by at a brisk pace. Our eyes meet. I salute in gratitude. He keeps walking—and smiles back.

Gilmore took my call at battalion. He burdened himself with my enthusiasm until he learned I wouldn't be returning to camp, at which point he sounded happy for the two of us. I talked briefly to a couple of the men, including Major Schiano, who received my profound thanks for his extraordinary effort. We wished each other the best of luck and ended the call.

I was due to depart An Khe late that same afternoon for Cam Ranh Bay. There I would spend two days processing out of country before taking a commercial airliner to Fort Lewis, Washington, where processing out of the military would continue.

Everything was going so fast it made my head hurt. Time was running out and there was so much more to do. I was supposed to return my rifle and ruck to supply and pick up my stored stateside duffle bag. I checked my watch. *Screw it.* Some Army bureaucrat was bound to stall me with paperwork or keep me waiting in line. To ensure I wouldn't miss my flight to Cam Ranh Bay, I forfeited my duffle and left my rifle and ruck inside the barrack.

I spent the next three nights at Cam Ranh Bay, in a barrack assigned to outbound military. Sleeping was difficult with all the noise and nervous energy in the room. Confrontations arose when some of the men segregated along racial lines, which only increased tensions.

Anyone scheduled to leave Vietnam had to change back into his stateside clothing issue. I couldn't comply because my stateside issue was still sitting in storage at An Khe. Company personnel were good enough to scrounge up the appropriate clothing for me, including a pair of used stateside boots that didn't quite fit. For no particular reason, I kept those boots for many years without ever wearing them. One day, while cleaning out the basement at home, I came across those old boots. Printed in black pen inside the boot uppers was the name and service number of the soldier who had once owned them. Curious, I brought out my Vietnam War Memorial directory and found an exact match. Now I knew why those boots were available to me at Cam Ranh Bay. They had belonged to a dead soldier, and I had worn them home.

Outbound personnel had to submit to a physical before getting a ticket back to the states. Scores of men in boxer shorts shuffled from one examination station to another getting checked out. One station looked like a voting booth covered in curtains. Only one man at a time was allowed inside. When it came to be my turn, I stepped in and found myself standing directly in front of a low-ranking soldier sitting on a chair.

"Pull down your drawers and milk your penis," he said.

"You serious?"

"Don't argue. I'm looking for pus."

On the day of my departure, groups of men waited outside for their scheduled flights, sitting or standing among rows of bench seats, all covered under canopy. I paced more than sat, and spoke to several of the men. It seemed like everyone had souvenirs and keepsakes to bring home. Due to my hasty exit from An Khe, all I salvaged was my cloth helmet cover and a black Cav scarf. Oh yeah, I also smuggled home in my boots one M-16 round and one AK-47 round.

When our freedom bird finally pulled up and steps were pushed to the plane's door, I felt a brief wave of dread, sure my name was about to be called over the loud speakers to rescind my DEROS. But then came the order to board, and I stepped into the plane and quietly took the nearest empty seat. Minutes later, a planeload of anxious soldiers sped down the runway. And only after the plane's wheels lifted off Vietnam soil did everyone let out a whoop and a holler...our Vietnam swan song!

DEROS, and Beyond

Engine problems forced our pilot to make an unscheduled land-ing in Japan. The stopover didn't particularly concern me if the delay was short. But it was not. We had to spend the night, which squeezed my already narrow timeline. The following day, we were airborne once again. After a short refueling stop in Alaska, our plane continued to Fort Lewis, Washington, and the U.S. Army Personnel Center headquartered there.

I had only one more day to process out of the Army or spend the next three months in uniform at some stateside military base. To help ensure that I wouldn't fall through the cracks, I became the squeaky wheel at the personnel center. And they provided the grease. Within twenty-four hours, I had a dress green uniform with insignias to wear off base, along with my separation orders and a plane voucher home.

Brothers Steve and Tom picked me up at the St. Louis airport and we headed straight for the nearest airport bar to celebrate my return. It was there I had my first encounter with a civilian who showed bias against veterans in uniform. A surly waitress carded me and then refused to accept my military I.D. She insisted on a driver's license, which I didn't have. The conversation heated after my brothers got involved, and only when the bar manager stepped in did things quiet down. He apologized to me and made things right.

My parents had by this time moved to Carbondale to help my brothers with their new businesses, and to be closer to the grand-kids. Having all the families living in the same town was wonder-ful. Mom and Dad put me up in their spare bedroom until I found a place of my own near campus. It felt strange sleeping on a mattress and box springs when I could have just as easily curled up on the carpeted floor.

Strange, too, was my first day of spring classes. Campus life seemed almost foreign to me. Considering I was fresh out of Vietnam, my current environment could not have been more different. In lecture hall, an attractive female sat next to me and we struck up a pleasant conversation. The next class day, we sat together again in the same seats and continued to hit it off. She asked about my deep tan, wondering if I got it in Florida over spring break. I said I had just returned from Vietnam and got my tan there, thinking she might be impressed. She was. On our next class day, she sat in another area of the lecture hall between two occupied seats.

My spring quarter grades were passing, but that's all. School still didn't hold my attention. I was too busy wildly enjoying the freedoms of civilian life, living self-indulgently, even to the exclusion of those I cared about, sad to say.

I chose not to attend summer classes. Instead I worked full-time at my brothers' growing businesses over that summer and beyond, never to look back. Aside from breaking my commitment to Colonel Bowen and Major Schiano, I have no other serious regrets for not finishing college. After thirty-four remarkable years in business, I retired as an equal partner.

Because my separation from the Army came so fast, my original form DD 214 (official separation papers) did not list two medals I believed I had earned: the Purple Heart and the Combat Infantry Badge. A clerk at the Fort Lewis personnel center said I should wait a few months before requesting an updated copy.

Years, not months, passed before I did just that, and what I found came as bittersweet. The Army awarded me two medals I didn't plan to receive: the Bronze Star for meritorious service and the Air Medal. Even though I was proud to receive them, I also wondered if I had done enough to deserve the honors. Missing from the list of awards was the Combat Infantry Badge awarded to all 11B MOS infantrymen (and other select MOS) involved in combat. My radio operator specialty precluded my getting a CIB, even though I fought in the field with an infantry company. I had mistakenly assumed that my infantry sergeant stripes came with a secondary 11B MOS. Circumstances may have been different had I requested the secondary distinction.

The most glaring omission in my record was the Purple Heart for wounds received in the firefight on 25 November 1968. For many years after the war I dismissed the oversight, avoiding that part of my past. But then I visited the Vietnam War Memorial in 1986 and my attitude changed. It was from that experience I felt compelled to write about my time in Vietnam. And through my writing, I came to accept my involvement in the war, if not the overlooked medal.

Minor though my wounds were, I did shed blood fighting in hostile action, and for that, I do qualify for the Purple Heart. However, at the time of the injury, it didn't occur to me that I had technically earned it. If only my company commander, Captain Talbott, had not declared that I would receive it, the Purple Heart may never have entered my mind in a serious way. But because I thought the award was part of my permanent record after I filled out the card for the doctor, I proudly told my family and friends as much. Years later, I had to take back my claim. That was difficult and more than a little embarrassing to me ("Hey everybody, you know that Purple Heart I told ya I got? Yeah, well, I was only kidding. Pretty funny, huh."").

Life will go on.

Vietnam War Memorial
October 1986

For many years after the war, Vietnam was only a distant thought. Like most veterans, I had a family and job to keep me busy, and some things were best left forgotten. Then in 1982 the Vietnam War Memorial was dedicated in Washington, D.C., and suddenly the war came back into America's consciousness. It is fair to say that Vietnam veterans liked the idea of a national memorial, but many disliked the final design, including me. I thought it resembled a black scar carved into dirt, thrusting yet another indignity upon us.

But something unexpected happened that changed my opinion. TV and print media showed images of veterans and non-veterans alike moved to tears at the Wall. Watching children touch their fathers' names and seeing veterans hug each other with tears in their eyes choked me up every time. But the memorial wasn't just a grim reminder of the past. There seemed to be a positive synergy at work between the war's dead and the living. Over fifty-eight thousand names etched into granite impacted visitors as no other memorial could. When tears flowed at the Wall, years of emotional wounds tended to scab over.

In September 1986, a friend and fellow veteran asked me to travel with him to the Wall. I really wanted to go but was afraid I would lose it in front of him and God only knows how many strangers. Stew Kath, a former Navy corpsman for Marine units in Vietnam, ultimately convinced me to accompany him. We would go together for mutual support.

At the end of October, Stew and I flew to D.C. and grabbed a cab to our hotel in Arlington, Virginia. The following morning, we took the metro to the National Mall. The Vietnam War Memorial was at the opposite end of the mall, and thus we began our long walk on a beautiful fall morning.

As we neared the monument, our conversation went from discussion to prattle to an anxious silence. *Too late to turn back now, I guess.* When over the final knoll the Wall came into view, our pace slowed to take it all in. My eyes locked onto the monument. Stew said, "Phil, look how big it is." A few steps more and he repeats himself.

The path in front of the memorial was busy with sightseers displaying varying reactions. Some stood in somber reflection. Some hugged in sad embrace. And then there were those clueless few who talked of little things.

Instead of following the path directly in front of the memorial, Stew and I instinctively took a path farther from it. Maybe we wanted a panoramic view. Or maybe it was something else.

From a distance, I focused all my attention on the Wall anticipating a strong emotional reaction. Instead, I felt only uncomfortably sad. *I can handle this*, I thought. Stew looked to be holding up as well.

We continued on path until it led to the Vietnam War Memorial statue located at the far corner of the monument. A small crowd was mingling around the bronze statue that portrayed three U.S. infantry soldiers. Each lifelike soldier was facing the Wall and each looked like he had just emerged from the jungles of Vietnam.

Stew drifted away to take pictures as I squeezed between spectators to the front of the statue. At the soldiers' feet I saw fresh flowers: a pink carnation, a white carnation, and a red rose. I was struck by the gesture. In honoring them, the donors seemed to be honoring me.

I began to stir inside.

When I finally looked up at the soldiers' faces, my eyes fixed on the eyes of the Caucasian figure standing in the forefront. They looked tired and immensely sad. I stared into its eyes until suddenly they became my eyes...and then the soldier became me. My throat tightened; my lips pursed. Tears welled up. I tried to control my unexpected reaction but could not. Turning from the crowd, I quickly escaped up a sidewalk to nearby Henry Bacon Drive and stopped at the curb to take in some deep breaths.

From across the street a lively game of flag football was in progress. Several young men, all in the prime of their lives, were engaged in the spirited contest. Watching them in action brought to mind images of other young men their age—men who, while in the prime of their lives, died engaged in man's ultimate contest.

I regained control over my emotions and returned down the sidewalk fully intending to avoid the statue. But when it came into view, a compelling force drew me to it. This time I quietly stood behind the crowd and focused my attention on a group of Boy Scouts huddled in front. The uniformed boys showed fascination at the bronze figures standing before them. One asked, "Is that a machine gun he's holding?" I was sorely tempted to answer his question but was afraid my emotions would betray me.

I very much wanted to say, "That's *me* you're looking at. I fought in Vietnam. Look closely boys...those are *my* eyes." Instead, I could only observe their keen interest in the foot soldiers.

Those boys didn't know it, but they were validating my involvement in the war in a way I never allowed myself before. They were giving me permission to set aside years of negative emotions I had come to feel over the conflict and replace them with a small sense of pride in my wartime effort. Those youngsters were not scorning, shunning, or ignoring the veterans in the way most Americans did for years during and following the war. They were not concerned about the politics of the conflict. Their young faces and innocent voices revealed their admiration for the American soldier who willingly risked it all. That admiration warmed me as much as it worried me, because they were indeed young and impressionable. Would they years later, and without introspection, don a different uniform, replacing their pledge to obey the scout law with a pledge "to preserve, protect and defend the Constitution of the United States?" And would they, if called to war by our government, truly be defending our country's vital interests or some ill-conceived strategic blunder? Time would tell.

I had avoided long enough the object I originally came to visit. Soon I was pacing in front of the war memorial, gazing at the thousands of names engraved in granite. At the base of the panels were mementos left by loved ones, fellow vets, and others. There were small American flags, pictures, letters, poetry—even a pair of combat boots. The significance of those tributes was both heartwarming and heart-wrenching to me.

Like so many people visiting the Wall, I wanted to locate the names of everyone I knew who was listed on it, of which there were many. The problem was I could not recall any last names—only a few nicknames, like Spider, Tex, Top, and Flip. But nicknames weren't listed on the Wall. Before leaving for Washington, I was lucky enough to contact two veterans who served in my old company. They helped me match a few given names to unforgettable faces.

From a nearby stand, I bought a thick directory and began my search. The first name on my list was on panel 37W, line 78. I located the panel and scanned the names until I found Spider's given name. Just then a park ranger happened by. I asked him where I might find the materials to make a rubbing. He didn't answer my question but instead asked me to point out the name. When I did, he reached into his breast pocket and pulled out a sheet of paper and a dark crayon. He put the paper over the indented letters and began to rub the crayon over it.

When finished, he politely handed me the rubbing, the crayon, and some extra paper. Another lump came to my throat.

I continued through the list, getting more emotional with each name that I found. When my searches had ended, I paced from one end of the Wall to the other, trying to make sense of my war, but the crowds distracted me. I needed room to collect my thoughts. That's when my legs took me over the swag chain, past the "keep off the grass" signs and to the solitude of that strong oak. At some point I rejoined society, but I could not come to grips with the war. Late afternoon, I left the Wall with a heavy heart and troubled spirit.

By that evening, my mood had brightened. Stew and I agreed to treat ourselves to dinner at a fine restaurant and took a cab to some fancy section of D.C. The first restaurant denied our entry because we weren't wearing dinner jackets. The next establishment did accommodate us, it being more interested in the color of our money than the cut of our cloth. Over Glenfiddich Scotch and raw oysters, followed by an expensive dinner and wine, Stew and I compared notes from earlier in the day. Stew lamented on his inability to remember the names of men he had aided on the battlefield. Some, he was certain, were listed on the Wall. I revealed to him that I had not yet come to terms with the war, the dead, and my involvement in it. Maybe I would go back to seek the answers, I said, but not tonight.

Morning hangovers dampened our enthusiasm to revisit the Wall but not from sticking to our original plans. We toured the Smithsonian on our last day in D.C. On our way back to the hotel that afternoon, dark clouds rolled in. By dinnertime, a steady rain began to fall, so we opted to dine at our hotel restaurant. During the meal, the topic of conversation returned to Vietnam. To his credit and my good fortune, Stew was a good listener. He helped me realize that I still carried some emotional baggage.

Back at the room, I grabbed a light jacket and told Stew I had to return to the Wall to take care of unfinished business. He looked out the window at the rain and said he'd rather stay in and read, if that was okay. I really wanted him to come along but couldn't bring myself to ask. Before leaving, he had me take his umbrella.

A cab picked me up at the front entrance to the hotel and took me to the same corner where those young men had played flag football the day before. By the time I walked to the memorial, I knew immediately this visit would be different from my first. Drizzling rain and black skies only intensified my dreary mood. The usual daily crowds had long left, and the weather would keep them away. Finally I was alone—alone with 58,000 eternal souls.

The memorial is dimly lit. Soft lights reflect off every other granite panel. In sharp contrast, the distant Washington Monument is ablaze in illumination.

The air is perfectly still. The only sound comes from raindrops tapping on the leaves and on the ground. I'm feeling anxious and begin breathing through my mouth, exhaling steamy clouds that hang in the air.

I pace in front of the Wall, much as an animal paces a cage. The more I pace, the more anxious and upset I become. I look into the sky hoping for divine intervention. In return, only raindrops splatter against my face; still clenched in my hand is the unopened umbrella. Being wet fits the occasion. It reminds me of all the times I was soaked to the bone in Nam. And I'm feeling alone and miserable. *How fucking appropriate.*

Leaning forward, I press my hands against the watery names. They draw me closer...closer, as if they have something to whisper. And then, suddenly, I'm back in Vietnam reliving the war, feeling all of its emotional extremes. The experience sends me into a turmoil, it is that vivid.

I push myself from the wall and try to blurt out all the hurt balled up inside me, but cannot. Something is holding me back. My gut is in a knot. My throat is tight. I can barely strain out the words, "I think I'm going crazy."

This is no time to be alone. Nearby I find a payphone.

"Can you come to the Wall, Stew?"

"What's the matter, Phil, you okay?"

"No, can you please come to the Wall?"

"Yeah, sure, of course. Hey, listen, Phil, take it easy, I'm on my way, don't go anywhere and don't do anything, I'm on my way, okay?"

"Okay."

Stew understands. He *will* come.

I'm back at the Wall again, nervously pacing in front of it. The rain has turned into a mist. A stranger in an overcoat appears in the distance. He stops to consider me, then turns and disappears.

More movement. Another figure emerges from the shadows. It's Stew. He has a look of uncertainty on his face, like he doesn't know what to expect. Frankly, neither do I. We walk tentatively toward each other. The closer we get the more emotional I become. By the time the gap closes between us, I have lost all self-control. I wrap my arms around Stew's jacket and break down in tears. Stew holds me. "It's all right, buddy. You're okay," he says over and over. All I can remember saying in return is, "The injustice of it all."

Within seconds I release Stew from my grip and notice he looks troubled. He turns away and steps toward the memorial to deal privately with his own emotions. In respect, I hang back and begin to analyze my shocking display.

What the hell just happened here?

Aside from some lingering sadness, I feel no embarrassment by my emotional outburst. And all the anxiety that was welling up inside me...gone, replaced by a great sense of relief.

I had experienced a cathartic event, a purging of my wartime demons—demons that had always prevented me from facing in full measure the asperities of Vietnam. The purging would continue over the years, kept alive through my writing on the subject. However, at long last I can say my journey ends here, but not without this one final admission. Ashamed as I am to say it, the truth is this: the tears I shed at the Wall were more for me than the dead I went to honor.

Minutes pass before Stew walks back from the memorial. With tears in his eyes and a nod of his head, he puts an arm over my shoulder.

And with that, we fade into the night.

Glossary of terms

AGENT ORANGE: defoliant/herbicide.

AIRMOBILE: people and/or material delivered by helicopter. Name was adopted by the 1st Air Cavalry (Airmobile).

AIR CAV: air cavalry.

AK-47: Russian made rifle used by the North Vietnamese Army and the Vietcong.

AMMO: ammunition.

AO: area of operations.

ARC LIGHT: B-52 Stratofortress air strike.

ARVN: Army of the Republic of Vietnam.

AWOL: absent without leave.

B-40 ROCKET: shoulder-held rocket propelled grenade launcher.

BASE CAMP: semi-permanent field headquarters.

BATTALION: organizational unit commanded by a lieutenant colonel.

BERM: low dirt wall fortification.

BIRD: any aircraft, usually helicopters.

BLUES: aero rifle platoon used for search and rescue.

BODY BAG: plastic bag used for retrieval of bodies on the battlefield.

BOOBY TRAP: explosive and non-explosive devices hidden by the enemy to kill or maim the unwary.

BEAUCOUP: much/many.

BUSH: expression for the jungle, or any remote area away from a base camp.

BRIGADE: organizational unit commanded by a colonel.

C-4: plastic explosive.

CAMO: camouflage.

CAR: CAR15 rifle, shorter version of the M16 assault rifle.

CAV: nickname for 1st Air Cavalry (Airmobile).

C & C: command and control helicopter.

CHARLIE/CHARLES/VICTOR CHARLES/VC: nicknames for Vietcong.

CHERRY: new in-country replacement.

CHICOM: a term describing a Chinese Communist or weapons manufactured in China.

CHIEU HOI: "Open Arms" program under which the government of South Vietnam offered amnesty to enemy defectors.

CHINOOK: CH-47 cargo and troop helicopter; also called "Shithook" or "Hook."

CHOPPER: any helicopter.

CIB: Combat Infantry Badge.

CIDG: (pronounced "sidgee") Civilian Irregular Defense Group.

CIGARS: supplies brought into the field by log birds.

CLAYMORE: U.S. antipersonnel land mine.

CLOSE AIR SUPPORT: air strikes against enemy targets that are close to friendly forces.

CO: commanding officer.

COBRA: AH-1G attack helicopter.

COMM, or COMMO: communications.

COMPANY: organizational unit commanded by a captain.

CP: command post.

CREW CHIEF: helicopter crewmember who maintains the aircraft.

C-RATIONS/C'S/C-RATS: canned meals used during military operations in Vietnam.

DAISY CUTTER: large bomb dropped by a C130 aircraft to clear an LZ.

DEROS: date eligible for return from overseas. The date a person's tour in Vietnam was estimated to end.

DI DI MAU/DI DI: move quickly.

DIME NICKEL: 105mm howitzer.

DINKY DAO: Americanized Vietnamese for "crazy".

DIVISION: organizational unit.

DMZ: demilitarized zone. A division line between North and South Vietnam at the seventeenth parallel as established by the Geneva Accords of 1954.

DOC: nickname for a medic.

DT: defensive target.

ELEPHANT GRASS: tall, sharp-edged grass.

EM: enlisted man.

ETS: estimated time of separation; date of departure from overseas duty station.

EXTRACTION: voluntary or involuntary withdrawal of troops from any operational area by helicopter.

F-4 PHANTOM: twin-engine, all-weather, tactical fighter-bomber.

FAC: forward air control.

FIELD OF FIRE: area that a weapon or group of weapons can cover effectively.

FIRE BASE/FIRE SUPPORT BASE/FB: artillery firing position.

FIRE FIGHT: exchange of small arms fire between opposing units.

FIRST TEAM: nickname for 1st Air Cavalry (Airmobile).

FLACK JACKET: heavy fiberglass-filled vest worn for protection from shrapnel.

FLARE: illumination projectile.

FNG: fucking new guy. A common name given to in-country arrivals.

FO: forward observer.

FRAG: common term for any grenade.

FREE FIRE ZONE: any area in which permission was not required prior to firing on targets.

FRIENDLIES: U.S. troops, allies, or any non-hostile civilians.

FRIENDLY FIRE: mistakenly directing fire on your own troops.

FSB: fire support base.

GI: general infantry. An infantry soldier.

GOOKS: slang expression brought to Vietnam by Korean War veterans. The term referred to anyone of Asian origin.

GREEN TRACERS: color left by the ammunition fired from enemy AK-47s to trace its path.

GRUNT: nickname for an infantryman in Vietnam, supposedly from the sound a soldier makes lifting up his rucksack.

GUERRILLA: resistance soldiers organized on a military or paramilitary basis.

GUERRILLA WARFARE: military operations conducted in enemy-held territory by predominantly indigenous, irregular forces.

GUNG HO: very enthusiastic.

GUNSHIP: armed helicopter or armed fixed-wing aircraft.

HE: high explosive.

HHC: headquarters and headquarters company.

H & I: harassment and interdicting artillery fire.

HOOCH (hootch): living quarters or a native hut.

HORN: radio operator.

HOT LZ/RED LZ: landing area where aircraft and/or soldiers are receiving enemy fire.

HQ: headquarters.

HUEY: nickname for the UH-series helicopters.

HUMPING HEAVY: foot soldier carrying a full pack in the field.

I CORPS: northernmost military region in South Vietnam.

II CORPS: Central Highlands military region in South Vietnam.

III CORPS: south-central military region between Saigon and the Highlands.

IV CORPS: southernmost military region in South Vietnam, located in the Mekong Delta.

INCOMING: receiving enemy mortar or rocket fire.

IN-COUNTRY: Vietnam.

INDIAN COUNTRY: area controlled by the enemy.

INSERTION: helicopter placement of combat troops in an operational area.

IN THE FIELD: any forward combat area or any area outside a populated area.

IRREGULARS: armed individuals or units not part of the regular armed forces.

KIA: killed in action.

KIT CARSON SCOUT: a North Vietnamese Regular or Viet Cong who defects and acts as a scout for U.S. troops.

KLICK: kilometer.

LBJ: Long Binh Jail (stockade).

LIFER: career soldier.

LINE 1: killed in action.

LINE 2: wounded in action.

LP: listening post. An infantry unit, usually squad or team size, that camps outside a perimeter overnight and listens for enemy movement.

LOACH/LOH: OH-6A light observation helicopter.

LOG BIRD: re-supply helicopter, usually a Huey.

LRRP (Lurp): long-range reconnaissance patrol.

LURPS: long-range reconnaissance patrol members. Also, a lightweight food packet consisting of a dehydrated meal named after the soldiers who most often used them.

LZ: landing zone.

M-16/Widow-Maker: standard American rifle used in Vietnam after 1966.

M-60: light machine gun carried by American troops in the field.

M-79: single-barreled grenade launcher used by infantry.

MACV (pronounced mack-vee): Military Assistance Command, Vietnam.

MAD MINUTE: concentrated fire of all weapons for sixty seconds at maximum rate.

MEDEVAC: medical evacuation by helicopter; also called an "evac" or "dustoff."

MIA: Missing In Action.

MIKE: microphone.

MONTAGNARDS/YARD: minority mountain people who lived in simple societies, and who joined forces with the Allies.

MOS: Military Occupational Specialty—one's job designation.

MPC: military payment currency used instead of US dollars.

NAPALM/NAPE: incendiary bombs used by American forces as a defoliant and antipersonnel weapon.

NCO: noncommissioned officer.

NINER-NINER: voice code used to call all radios on a given frequency.

NLF: National Liberation Front, officially the National Front for the Liberation of the South.

NVA: North Vietnamese Army.

OJT: on the job training.

P-38/JOHN WAYNE: can opener for canned C-rations.

PENNY: radio code for an enlisted man.

PFC: Private First Class.

PLATOON: organizational unit commanded by a 1st or 2nd lieutenant.

POINT MAN: a soldier who leads a unit in the bush; arguably the most dangerous job in a rifle company.

PONCHO LINER: camouflaged nylon liner inserted into the military rain poncho; used as a blanket.

POP SMOKE: smoke grenade to mark an area.

PRC-25 (Prick): short-range, man-pack portable, frequency modulated (fm) receiver-transmitter used to provide two-way voice communication.

Frequency range:
WW band. 30.00 to 52.95 mc.
High band. 53.00 to 75.95 mc.
Number of channels: 920.

Transmitter output power: ~ 1.5 to 2.0 watts.
Type of squelch: Tone operated.
Distance range: Five miles

Types of antennas:
Short antenna. Three foot long, semi-rigid steel tape.
Long antenna. Ten foot long, multi-section whip.

Power source: Dry Battery
Battery life: Twenty hours with a 9 to1 receive-transmit ratio.

PT: physical training.

PUSH: radio frequency.

RECON: reconnaissance.

REDLEG: artillery battery.

REMF: rear echelon motherfucker. Nickname given to men serving in the rear by front-line soldiers.

RF: reference point on a map

ROCK 'N' ROLL: an M-16 assault rifle fired on full automatic.

RPG: enemy rocket-propelled grenade.

R & R: rest-and-recreation vacation.

RTO: radiotelephone operator.

RUCK/RUCKSACK: backpack used by infantrymen in Vietnam.

RVN: Republic of Vietnam (South Vietnam).

SAPPERS: enemy demolition commandos.

SEARCH AND DESTROY/CLEAR: military operations designed to sweep through areas to destroy/clear the enemy.

SHORT TIMER: individual with little time remaining in Vietnam.

SITREP: situation report.

SLICK: helicopter used to move troops.

SOP: Standard Operating Procedure.

SORTIE: aircraft making one takeoff and landing to conduct a mission.

SPOOKY/PUFF THE MAGIC DRAGON: AC-47 Gunship.

SQUAD: basic organizational unit led by a sergeant.

SNAFU: situation normal all fucked up.

STAND-DOWN: period of rest and refitting in which all operational activity, except for security, is halted.

TET: Vietnamese Lunar New Year holiday period.

THUMPER: M-79 grenade launcher, so called because it made a hollow "thump" noise when fired.

TOC: tactical operations center. Tactical operations bunker containing radios and maps, and where the "Old Man" bunked.

UPCON: under operational control. A military unit moving under control to another unit.

VIETCONG or VC: Communist forces fighting the South Vietnamese government.

WIA: wounded in action.

WP/WILLIE PETER/WHISKEY PAPA: nicknames for white phosphorus.

WO: Warrant Officer.

(THE) WORLD: the United States.

XO: executive officer. Second in command.

21877430R00135

Made in the USA
Charleston, SC
03 September 2013